THE

MAN OF UZ,

AND

OTHER POEMS.

BY

MRS. L. H. SIGOURNEY.

HARTFORD:
WILLIAMS, WILEY & WATERMAN.
1862.

PREFACE.

The arrogance of attempting a parody on the most ancient and sublime poem in the Inspired Volume, is not mine. The great pleasure enjoyed in its perusal from early years, had occasionally prompted metrical imitations of isolated passages. These fragmentary effusions, recently woven together, are here presented, with the hope that as wandering streams are traced to their original fountain, some heart may thus be led to the history of the stricken and sustained Patriarch, with more studious research, purer delight, or a deeper spirit of devotion.

L. H. S.

Hartford, Conn., November 5th, 1862.

CONTENTS.

PAGE.

PREFACE, ... 3

THE MAN OF UZ, ... 9

THE RURAL LIFE IN NEW ENGLAND,

CANTO FIRST, ... 59

CANTO SECOND, ... 91

CANTO THIRD, ... 109

IN MEMORIAM.

1859.

REV. DR. T. M COOLEY, ... 147

MADAM OLIVIA PHELPS, ... 149

MARTHA AGNES BONNER, ... 151

MADAM WHITING, ... 153

DENISON OLMSTED, LL. D., ... 155

HERBERT FOSS, ... 157

MRS. CHARLES N. CADWALLADER, ... 159

REV. DR. JAMES W. ALEXANDER, ... 161

MRS. JOSEPH MORGAN, ... 163

ALICE BECKWITH, ... 165

MARY SHIPMAN DEMING, ... 167

1860.

	Page.
Rev. Dr. F. W. Hatch,	169
Mrs. Payne,	171
Mrs. Mary Mildenstein Robertson,	173
Madam Williams,	175
Mr. Samuel Ogden,	177
Mr. George Beach,	179
Miss Margaret C. Brown,	181
Miss Frances Wyman Tracy,	183
Deacon Normand Smith,	185
Mrs. Helen Tyler Beach,	187
Mrs. Elizabeth Harris,	189
Miss Anna M. Seymour,	191
Caleb Hazen Talcott,	193

1861.

Miss Jane Penelope Whiting,	195
Miss Anna Freeman,	197
Madam Pond,	199
Annie Seymour Robinson,	201
Mrs. Georgiana Ives Comstock,	203
Wentworth Alexander,	206
Mrs. Harvey Seymour,	208
Mrs. Frederick Tyler,	211
Miss Laura Kingsbury,	213
Govenor and Mrs. Trumbull,	214
Mrs. Emily Ellsworth,	218
Rev. Dr. Stephen Jewitt,	220
Miss Delia Woodruff Godding,	222
Miss Sara K. Taylor,	224
Mr. John Warburton,	226

	Page.
Rev. Henry Albertson Post,	228
Miss Caroline L. Griffin,	230
Mr. Normand Burr,	232
Hon. Thomas S. Williams,	234
Col. H. L. Miller,	237
1862.	
Col. Samuel Colt,	239
Madam Hannah Lathrop,	242
Henrietta Selden Colt,	244
The Little Brothers,	247
Mr. D. F. Robinson,	249
Mr. Samuel Tudor,	251
Henry Howard Comstock,	254
Rev. Dr. David Smith,	256
Miss Emily B. Parish,	258
Harriet Allen Ely,	260
Miss Catharine Ball,	261
Mrs. Morris Collins,	263
Mrs. Margaret Walbridge,	265
The Brothers Buell,	267
Mr. Phillip Ripley,	269
Richard Ely Collins,	271
Miss Elizabeth Brinley,	273
Mr. John A. Taintor,	275

THE MAN OF UZ.

A JOYOUS FESTIVAL.—
The gathering back
Of scattered flowrets to the household wreath.
Brothers and sisters from their sever'd homes
Meeting with ardent smile, to renovate
The love that sprang from cradle memories
And childhood's sports, and whose perennial stream
Still threw fresh crystals o'er the sands of life.
—Each bore some treasured picture of the past,
Some graphic incident, by mellowing time
Made beautiful, while ever and anon,
Timbrel and harp broke forth, each pause between.
Banquet and wine-cup, and the dance, gave speed
To youthful spirits, and prolong'd the joy.

The patriarch father, with a chasten'd heart
Partook his children's mirth, having God's fear
Ever before him. Earnestly he brought
His offerings and his prayers for every one
Of that beloved group, lest in the swell

And surging superflux of happiness
They might forget the Hand from whence it came,
Perchance, displease the Almighty.
Many a care
Had he that wealth creates. Not such as lurks
In heaps metallic, which the rust corrodes,
But wealth that fructifies within the earth
Whence cometh bread, or o'er its surface roves
In peaceful forms of quadrupedal life
That thronging round the world's first father came
To take their names, 'mid Eden's tranquil shades,
Ere sin was born.
Obedient to the yoke,
Five hundred oxen turn'd the furrow'd glebe
Where agriculture hides his buried seed
Waiting the harvest hope, while patient wrought
An equal number of that race who share
The labor of the steed, without his praise.
—Three thousand camels, with their arching necks,
Ships of the desert, knelt to do his will,
And bear his surplus wealth to distant climes,
While more than twice three thousand snowy sheep
Whitened the hills. Troops of retainers fed
These flocks and herds, and their subsistence drew
From the same lord,—so that this man of Uz
Greater than all the magnates of the east,
Dwelt in old time before us.
True he gave,
And faithfully, the hireling his reward,

Counting such justice 'mid the happier forms
Of Charity, which with a liberal hand
He to the sad and suffering poor dispensed.
Eyes was he to the blind, and to the lame
Feet, while the stranger and the traveller found
Beneath the welcome shelter of his roof
The blessed boon of hospitality.

To him the fatherless and widow sought
For aid and counsel. Fearlessly he rose
For those who had no helper. His just mind
Brought stifled truth to light, disarm'd the wiles
Of power, and gave deliverance to the weak.
He pluck'd the victim from the oppressor's grasp,
And made the tyrant tremble.
To his words
Men listened, as to lore oracular,
And when beside the gate he took his seat
The young kept silence, and the old rose up
To do him honor. After his decree
None spake again, for as a prince he dwelt
Wearing the diadem of righteousness,
And robed in that respect which greatness wins
When leagued with goodness, and by wisdom crown'd.
The grateful prayers and blessings of the souls
Ready to perish, silently distill'd
Upon him, as he slept.
So as a tree
Whose root is by the river's brink, he grew

And flourish'd, while the dews like balm-drops hung
All night upon his branches.
Yet let none
Of woman born, presume to build his hopes
On the worn cliff of brief prosperity,
Or from the present promise, predicate
The future joy. The exulting bird that sings
Mid the green curtains of its leafy nest
His tuneful trust untroubled there to live,
And there to die, may meet the archer's shaft
When next it spreads the wing.
The tempest folds
O'er the smooth forehead of the summer noon
Its undiscover'd purpose, to emerge
Resistless from its armory, and whelm
In floods of ruin, ere the day decline.

Lightning and sword!
Swift messengers, and sharp,
Reapers that leave no gleanings. In their path
Silence and desolation fiercely stalk.
—O'er trampled hills, and on the blood-stain'd plains
There is no low of kine, or bleat of flocks,
The fields are rifled, and the shepherds slain.

The Man of Uz, who stood but yestermorn
Above all compeers,—clothed with wealth and power,
To day is poorer than his humblest hind.

A whirlwind from the desert!
All unwarn'd
Its fury came. Earth like a vassal shook.
Majestic trees flew hurtling through the air
Like rootless reeds.
There was no time for flight.
Buried in household wrecks, all helpless lay
Masses of quivering life.
Job's eldest son
That day held banquet for their numerous line
At his own house. With revelry and song,
One moment in the glow of kindred hearts
The lordly mansion rang, the next they lay
Crush'd neath its ruins.
He,—the childless sire,
Last of his race, and lonely as the pine
That crisps and blackens 'neath the lightning shaft
Upon the cliff, with such a rushing tide
The mountain billows of his misery came,
Drove they not Reason from her beacon-hold?
Swept they not his strong trust in Heaven away?

List,—list,—the sufferer speaks.
"The Lord who gave
Hath taken away,—and blessed be His name."

Oh Patriarch!—teach us, mid this changeful life
Not to mistake the ownership of joys
Entrusted to us for a little while,

But when the Great Dispenser shall reclaim
His loans, to render them with praises back,
As best befits the indebted.
                                        Should a tear
Moisten the offering, He who knows our frame
And well remembereth that we are but dust,
Is full of pity.
                                        It was said of old
Time conquer'd Grief. But unto me it seems
That Grief overmastereth Time. It shows how wide
The chasm between us, and our smitten joys
And saps the strength wherewith at first we went
Into life's battle. We perchance, have dream'd
That the sweet smile the sunbeam of our home
The prattle of the babe the Spoiler seiz'd,
Had but gone from us for a little while,—
And listen'd in our fallacy of hope
At hush of eve for the returning step
That wake the inmost pulses of the heart
To extasy,—till iron-handed Grief
Press'd down the *nevermore* into our soul,
Deadening us with its weight.
                                        The man of Uz
As the slow lapse of days and nights reveal'd
The desolation of his poverty
Felt every nerve that at the first great shock
Was paralyzed, grow sensitive and shrink
As from a fresh-cut wound. There was no son
To come in beauty of his manly prime

With words of counsel and with vigorous hand
To aid him in his need, no daughter's arm
To twine around him in his weariness,
Nor kiss of grandchild at the even-tide
Going to rest, with prayer upon its lips.

Still a new trial waits.
The blessed health
Heaven's boon, thro' which with unbow'd form we bear
Burdens and ills, forsook him. Maladies
Of fierce and festering virulence attack'd
His swollen limbs. Incessant, grinding pains
Laid his strength prostrate, till he counted life
A loathed thing. Dire visions frighted sleep
That sweet restorer of the wasted frame,
And mid his tossings to and fro, he moan'd
Oh, when shall I arise, and Night be gone!

Despondence seized him. To the lowliest place
Alone he stole, and sadly took his seat
In dust and ashes.
She, his bosom friend
The sharer of his lot for many years,
Sought out his dark retreat. Shuddering she saw
His kingly form like living sepulchre,
And in the maddening haste of sorrow said
God hath forgotten.
She with him had borne
Unuttered woe o'er the untimely graves
Of all whom she had nourished,—shared with him

The silence of a home that hath no child,
The plunge from wealth to want, the base contempt
Of menial and of ingrate;—but to see
The dearest object of adoring love
Her next to God, a prey to vile disease
Hideous and loathsome, all the beauty marred
That she had worshipped from her ardent youth
Deeming it half divine, she could not bear,
Her woman's strength gave way, and impious words
In her despair she uttered.
But her lord
To deeper anguish stung by her defect
And rash advice, reprovingly replied
Pointing to Him who meeteth out below
Both good and evil in mysterious love,
And she was silenced.
What a sacred power
Hath hallow'd Friendship o'er the nameless ills
That throng our pilgrimage. Its sympathy,
Doth undergird the drooping, and uphold
The foot that falters in its miry path.
It grows more precious, as the hair grows grey.
Time's alchymy that rendereth so much dross
Back for our gay entrustments, shows more pure
The perfect essence of its sanctity,
Gold unalloyed.
How doth the cordial grasp,
Of hands that twined with ours in school days, now
Delight us as our sunbeam nears the west,

Soothing, perchance our self-esteem with proofs
That 'mid all faults the good have loved us still,
And quickening with redoubled energy
To do or suffer.
The three friends of Job
Who in the different regions where they dwelt
Teman, and Naamah and the Shuhite land,
Heard tidings of his dire calamity,
Moved by one impulse, journey'd to impart
Their sorrowing sympathy.
Yet when they saw
Him fallen so low, so chang'd that scarce a trace
Remained to herald his identity
Down by his side upon the earth, they sate
Uttering no language save the gushing tear,—
Spontaneous homage to a grief so great.

Oh Silence, born of Wisdom! we have felt
Thy fitness, when beside the smitten friend
We took our place. The voiceless sympathy
The tear, the tender pressure of the hand
Interpreted more perfectly than words
The purpose of our soul.
We *speak* to err,
Waking to agony some broken chord
Or bleeding nerve that slumbered. Words are weak,
When God's strong discipline doth try the soul;
And that deep silence was more eloquent
Than all the pomp of speech.

Yet the long pause
Of days and nights, gave scope for troubled thought
And their bewildered minds unskillfully
Launching all helmless on a sea of doubt
Explored the cause for which such woes were sent,
Forgetful that this mystery of life
Yields not to man's solution. Passing on
From natural pity to philosophy
That deems Heaven's judgments penal, they inferr'd
Some secret sin unshrived by penitence,
That drew such awful visitations down.
While studying thus the *wherefore*, with vain toil
Of painful cogitation, lo! a voice
Hollow and hoarse, as from the mouldering tomb,

"Perish the day in which I saw the light!
The day when first my mother's nursing care
Sheltered my helplessness. Let it not come
Into the number of the joyful months,
Let blackness stain it and the shades of death
Forever terrify it.
For it cut
Not off as an untimely birth my span,
Nor let me sleep where the poor prisoners hear
No more the oppressor, where the wicked cease
From troubling and the weary are at rest.
Now as the roar of waves my sorrows swell,
And sighs like tides burst forth till I forget
To eat my bread. That which I greatly feared

Hath come upon me. Not in heedless pride
Nor wrapped in arrogance of full content
I dwelt amid the tide of prosperous days,
And yet this trouble came."
With mien unmoved
The Temanite reprovingly replied:
"Who can refrain longer from words, even though
To speak be grief? Thou hast the instructor been
Of many, and their model how to act.
When trial came upon them, if their knees
Bow'd down, thou saidst, "be strong," and they obey'd.
But now it toucheth thee and thou dost shrink,
And murmuring, faint. The monitor forgets
The precepts he hath taught. Is this thy faith,
Thy confidence, the uprightness of thy way?
Whoever perish'd being innocent?
And when were those who walk'd in righteous ways
Cut off? How oft I've seen that those who sow
The seeds of evil secretly, and plow
Under a veil of darkness, reap the same.

In visions of the night, when deepest sleep
Falls upon men, fear seiz'd me, all my bones
Trembled, and every stiffening hair rose up.
A spirit pass'd before me, but I saw
No form thereof. I knew that there it stood,
Even though my straining eyes discern'd it not.
Then from its moveless lips a voice burst forth,
"Is man more just than God? Is mortal man

More pure than He who made him?
Lo, he puts
No trust in those who serve him, and doth charge
Angels with folly. How much less in them
Dwellers in tents of clay, whose pride is crush'd
Before the moth. From morn to eve they die
And none regard it."
So despise thou not
The chastening of the Almighty, ever just,
For did thy spirit please him, it should rise
More glorious from the storm-cloud, all the earth
At peace with thee, new offspring like the grass
Cheering thy home, and when thy course was done
Even as a shock of corn comes fully ripe
Into the garner should thy burial be
Belov'd and wept of all."

Mournful arose
The sorrowful response.
"Oh that my grief
Were in the balance laid by faithful hands
And feeling hearts. To the afflicted soul
Friends should be comforters. But mine have dealt
Deceitfully, as fails the shallow brook
When summer's need is sorest.
Did I say
Bring me a gift? or from your flowing wealth
Give solace to my desolate penury?
Or with your pitying influence neutralize
My cup of scorn poured out by abject hands?

That thus ye mock me with contemptuous words
And futile arguments, and dig a pit
In which to whelm the man you call a friend?
Still darkly hinting at some heinous sin
Mysteriously concealed?
                                        Writes conscious guilt
No transcript on the brow? Hangs it not out
Its signal there, altho' it seem to hide
'Neath an impervious shroud?
                                        Look thro' the depths
Of my unshrinking eye, deep, deep within.
What see ye there? what gives suspicion birth?
As longs the laborer for the setting sun,
Watching the lengthening shadows that foretell
The time of rest, yet day by day returns
To the same task again, so I endure
Wearisome nights and months of burdening woe.
I would not alway live this loathed life
Whose days are vanity. Soon shall I sleep
Low in the dust, and when the morning comes
And thro' its curtaining mists ye seek my face
I shall not be."

                                        Earnest the Shuhite spake,
"How long shall these thy words, like eddying winds
Fall empty on the ear?
                                        Doth God pervert
Justice and judgment? If thy way was pure,
Thy supplication from an upright heart

He would awake and make thy latter end
More blest than thy beginning.
For inquire
Of ancient times, of History's honor'd scroll
And of the grey-hair'd fathers, if our words
Seem light, we who were born but yesterday.
Ask them and they shall teach thee, as the rush,
Or as the flag forsaken of the pod,
So shall the glory of the hypocrite
Fade in its greenness.
Tho' his house may seem
Awhile to flourish, it shall not endure.
Even tho' he grasp it with despairing strength
It shall deceive his trust and pass away,
As fleets the spider's filmy web. Behold
God will not cast away the perfect man
Nor help the evil doer."

In low tones,
Sepulchral, and with pain, the sufferer spake,
"I know that this is truth, but how can man
Be just with God? How shall he dare contend
With Him who stretches out the sky and treads
Upon the mountain billows of the sea,
And sealeth up the stars?
Array'd in strength,
He passeth by me, but I see Him not.
I hear His chariot-wheels, yet fear to ask
Where goest Thou?

If I, indeed, were pure,
And perfect, like the model ye see fit
To press upon me with your sharpest words,
I would not in mine arrogance arise
And reason with Him, but all humbly make
Petition to my Judge.

If there were one
To shield me from His terrors, and to stand
As mediator, I might dare to ask
Why didst Thou give this unrequested boon
Of life, to me, unhappy? My few days
Are swifter than a post. As the white sail
Fades in the mist, as the strong eagle's wing
Leaves no receding trace, they flee away,
They see no good.

Hath not Thy mighty hand
Fashion'd and made this curious form of clay,
Fenc'd round with bones and sinews, and inspired
By a mysterious soul? Oh be not stern
Against Thy creature, as the Lion marks
His destin'd prey.

Relent and let me take
Comfort a little, ere I go the way
Whence I return no more, to that far land
Of darkness and the dreary shades of death."

Scarce had he ceas'd ere Zophar's turbid thoughts
Made speed to answer.

"Shall a tide of talk

Wash out transgression? If thou choose to set
The truth at nought, must others hold their peace?
Hast thou not boasted that thy deeds and thoughts
Were perfect in the almighty Maker's sight?
Canst thou by searching find out God? Behold
Higher than heaven it is, what canst thou do?
Deeper than deepest hell, what canst thou know?
Why wilt thou ignorantly deem thyself
Unblamed before Him?
                                Oh that He would speak,
And put to shame thine arrogance.
                                His glance
Discerns all wickedness, all vain pretence
To sanctity and wisdom. Were thine heart
Rightly prepared, and evil put away
From that and from thy house, then shouldst thou lift
Thy spotless face, clear as the noon-day sun
Stedfast and fearless. Yea, thou shouldst forget
Thy misery, as waters that have past
Away forever.
                                Thou shouldst be secure
And dig about thee and take root, and rest,
While those who scorn thee now, with soul abased,
Should make their suit unto thee.
                                But the eyes
Of wicked men shall fail, and as the groan
Of him who giveth up the ghost, shall be
Their frustrate hope."

Dejectedly, as one
Who wearied in a race, despairs to reach
The destined goal, nor yet consents to leave
His compeers masters of an unwon field.
Job said,—

"No doubt ye think to have attained
Monopoly of knowledge, and with you
Wisdom shall die. This modesty of creed
Befits ye well. Yet what have ye alledg'd
Unheard before? what great discoveries made?
Who knoweth not such things as ye have told?
Despised am I by those who call'd me friend
In prosperous days. Like a dim, waning lamp
About to be extinguished am I held
By the dull minds of those who dwell at ease.
Weak reasoners that ye are, ye have essay'd
To speak for God. Suppose ye He doth need
Such advocacy? whose creative hand
Holdeth the soul of every living thing,
And breath of all mankind?

He breaketh down,
And who can build again? Princes and kings
Are nothing in his sight. Disrobed of power
Ceaseless they wander and He heedeth not.
Those whom the world have worship'd seem as fools.
He lifteth up the nations at His will,
Or sweeps them with his lightest breath away
Like noteless atoms.

Silence is for you
The truest wisdom. Creatures that ye count
Inferior to yourselves, who in thin air
Spread the light wing, or thro' the waters glide,
Or roam the earth, might teach if ye would hear
And be instructed by them.
Hold your peace!
Even tho' He slay me I will trust in Him
For He is my salvation, He alone;
At whose dread throne no hypocrite shall dare
To stand, or answer.
Man, of woman born
Is of few days, and full of misery.
Forth like a flower he comes, and is cut down,
He fleeth like a shadow. What is man
That God regardeth him? The forest tree
Fell'd by the woodman may have hope to live
And sprout again, and thro' the blessed touch
Of waters at the root put forth new buds
And tender branches like a plant. But man
Shorn of his strength, doth waste away and die,
He giveth up the ghost and where is he?
As slides the mountain from its heaving base
Hurling its masses o'er the startled vale,
As the rent rock resumes its place no more,
As the departed waters leave no trace
Save the groov'd channels where they held their course
Among the fissur'd stones, his form of dust
With its chang'd countenance, is sent away
And all the honors that he sought to leave

Behind him to his sons, avail him not."
He ceas'd and Eliphaz rejoin'd,
"A man
Of wisdom dealeth not in empty words
That like the east wind stirs the unsettled sands
To profitless revolt. Thou dost decry
Our speech and proudly justify thyself
Before thy God. He to whose searching eye
Heavens' pure immaculate ether seems unclean.
Ask of tradition, ask the white hair'd men
Much older than thy father, since to us
Thou deign'st no credence. Say they not to thee,
All, as with one consent, the wicked man
Travaileth with fruitless pain, a dreadful sound
Forever in his ears; the mustering tramp
Of hostile legions on the distant cloud,
A far-off echo from the woe to come?
Such is his lot who sinfully contends
Against the just will of the Judging One,
Lifting his puny arm in rebel pride
And rushing like a madman on his doom.
The wealth he may have gathered shall dissolve
And turn to ashes mid devouring flame.
His branch shall not be green, but as the vine
Casteth her unripe grapes, as thro' the leaves
Of rich and lustrous hue, the olive buds
Untimely strew the ground, shall be his trust
Who in the contumacy of his pride
Would fain deceive both others and himself."

To whom, the Man of Uz,—
"These occult truths
If such ye deem them, I have heard before;
Oh miserable comforters! I too
Stood but your soul in my soul's stead, could heap
Vain, bitter words, and shake my head in scorn.
But I would study to assuage your pain,
And solace shed upon your stricken hearts
With balm-drops of sweet speech.
Yet, as for me,
I speak and none regard, or drooping sit
In mournful silence, and none heed my woe.
They smite me on the cheek reproachfully,
And slander me in secret, though my cause
And witness rest with the clear-judging Heaven.
My record is on high.
Oh Thou, whose hand
Hath thus made desolate all my company,
And left me a poor, childless man—behold
They who once felt it pride to call me friend,
Make of my name a by-word, which was erst
Like harp or tabret to their venal lip.
Mine eye is dim with grief, my wasted brow
Furrow'd with wrinkles.
Soon I go the way
Whence I shall not return. The grave, my house,
Is ready for me. In its mouldering clay
My bed I make, and say unto the worm
Thou art my sister."

With unpitying voice
Not comprehending Job, the Shuhite spake.
" How long ere thou shalt make an end of words
So profitless and vain? Thou dost account
Us vile as beasts. But shall the stable earth
With all its rocks and mountains be removed
For thy good pleasure?

See, the light forsake
The wicked man. Darkness and loneliness
Enshroud his dwelling-place. His path shall be
Mid snares and traps, and his own counsel fail
To guide him safely. By the heel, the gin
Shall seize him, and the robber's hand prevail
To rifle and destroy his treasure hoard.
Secret misgivings feed upon his strength,
And terrors waste his courage. He shall find
In his own tabernacle no repose,
Nor confidence. His withering root shall draw
No nutriment, and the unsparing ax
Cut off his branches. From a loathing world
He shall be chased away, and leave behind
No son or nephew to bear up his name
Among the people. No kind memories
Shall linger round his ashes, or refresh
The hearts of men. They who come after him
Shall be astonish'd at his doom, as they
Who went before him, view'd it with affright.
Such is the lot of those who know not God
Or wickedly renounce Him."

Earnestly
Replied the suffering man,
"Ye vex my soul
And break it into pieces. These ten times
Have ye reproach'd me, without sense of shame
Or touch of sympathy. If I have err'd
As without witness ye essay to prove
'Tis my concern, not yours.
But yet, how vain
To speak of wrong, or plead the cause of truth
Before the unjust.
Can ye not understand
God in his wisdom hath afflicted me?
His hand hath reft away my crown and stripp'd
Me of my glory. Kindred blood vouchsafes
No aid or solace in my deep distress.
Estrang'd and far away, like statues cold
Brethren and kinsfolk stand. Familiar friends
Frown on me as a stranger. They who dwell
In my own house and eat my bread, despise me.
I call'd my own tried servant, but he gave
No answer or regard. My maidens train'd
For household service, to perform my will
Count me an alien;—even with my wife
My voice hath lost its power. Young children rise
And push away my feet and mock my words.
Yea, the best loved, most garner'd in my heart
Do turn against me as a thing abhorr'd.
Have pity, pity on me, oh my friends!
The hand of God hath smitten me.

I know
That my Redeemer liveth, and shall stand
At last upon the earth, and though in death
Worms shall destroy this body, in my flesh
Shall I see God."

This glorious burst of faith
Springing from depths of misery and pain
Awed them a moment, like the lightning's flash,
Cleaving the cloud. But gathering strength again,
They sought the conflict.
"Thou, who art so wise,
Hast thou not learn'd how baseless is the joy
And boasting of the hypocrite? His head
Up to the heavens in excellence and pride
May seem to mount, yet shall he swiftly fall
Leaving no trace. Though still he toils to keep
His sin a secret from his fellow-men,
Like a sweet, stolen morsel, hiding it
Under his tongue, yet shall the veil be rent.
God's fearful judgments shall make evident
What he hath done in darkness. Vipers' tongues
And the dire poison of the asp, shall be
His recompense. Terrors shall strike him through,
An inward fire of sharp remorse, unblown
By mortal hand, shall on his vitals feed,
And all his strength consume. His wealth shall fleet,
And they who trusted to become his heirs
Embrace a shadow, for his goods shall flow

Away, as the false brook forsakes its sands.
This is the portion of the hypocrite,
The heritage appointed him by God."

To Zophar answered Job,—
"Hear ye my speech,
And when 'tis done, mock on. Not unto man
Is my complaint. For were it so, my heart
Would sink in darker depths of hopeless woe.
Say ye that earth's 'prosperity' rewards
The righteous man? Why do the wicked live,
Grow old, and magnify themselves in power?
Their offspring flourish round them, their abodes
Are safe from fear. Their cattle multiply
And widely o'er the hills and pastures green
Wander their healthful herds. Forth like a flock
They send their little ones, with dance and song,
Tabret and harp. They spend their days in wealth
And sink to slumber in the quiet grave.
Yet unto God they said, Depart from us,
For we desire no knowledge of thy ways.
Why should we serve the Almighty? Who is he?
And what our profit if we pray to Him?

Close by these impious ones lies down to sleep,
One in the strength and glory of his prime,
Whom sorrow never touch'd, nor age impair'd;
And still another, wan misfortune's child,
Nurtur'd in bitterness, who never took

His meat with pleasure. Side by side they rest
On Death's oblivious pillow. Do ye say
Their varied lot below, mark'd their deserts?
In retribution just?

But as for you
With eyes so sharp for your own selfish ends,
Who by the wayside ask where'er ye go,
"*Where is the dwelling of the prince?* and seek
Gain more than godliness, I know full well
Your deep contempt for one too poor to bribe
Your false allegiance, and the unkind device
Ye wrongfully imagine.
Will ye teach
Knowledge to God? Doth He not wisely judge
The highest? and reserve the sons of guilt
For the destruction that awaiteth them?"

In quick rejoinder, Eliphaz replied,
" What is thy fancied goodness in the sight
Of the Almighty? Is it gain to Him
If thou art righteous? Would it add to Him
Gladness or glory, that thy ways should be
What thou call'st perfect?
Rather turn thine eyes
Upon the record of thy sins, and see
Their countless number.
Hast thou taken a pledge
From thy poor brother's hand? or reft away

4

The garment from the shivering? or withheld
Bread from the hungry? or the widow sent
Empty away? not given the weary soul
What it implored? nor bound the broken arm
Of the forsaken fatherless?
                    For this
Have snares beset thee? and a secret fear
Dismay'd thy spirit? and a rayless night
Shut over thee?
                    Look to the height of heaven,
Above the utmost star. Is not God there?
Think'st thou that aught can intercept His sight
Or bar His righteous judgment? He who makes
The thickest clouds His footstool, when He walks
Upon the circuit of the highest heavens?
Acquaint thyself with Him and be at peace,
Return to Him, and He shall build thee up.
Take thou His precepts to thine inmost heart
That thy lost blessings may revisit thee.
Put far away thy foster'd sins, and share
The swelling flood-tide of prosperity.
Thou shalt have silver at thy will, and gold,
The gold of Ophir in thy path shall lie
As stones that pave the brooks.
                    Make thou thy prayer,
And pay thy vows, and He will hear thy voice
And give thee light, and thy desires confirm:
For He will save the humble and protect
The innocent and still deliver those
Whose hands are pure."

To whom, the Man of Uz,

"Oh that I knew where I might find my Judge,
That I might press even to His seat, and plead
My cause before Him. Would He strike me dumb
With His great power? Nay,—rather would he give
Strength to the weakness that would answer Him.
Lo! I go forward,—but He is not there,—
And backward, yet my eyes perceive Him not.
On the left hand, His works surround me still,
But He is absent,—on the right, I gaze,
Yet doth He hide Himself.
But well He knows
My way, and when the time of trial's o'er,
And the refining fire hath purg'd the dross,
I shall come forth as gold. My feet have kept
The path appointed, nor from His commands
Unduly swerved, for I have prized His word
More than my needful food.
Yet He performs
What His wise counsel hath decreed for me,
Though sometimes sinks my soften'd heart beneath
The terror of His stroke.
There are, who seize
With violence whate'er their eyes desire;
Gorging themselves upon the stolen flock .
And leaving desolate the rifled hut
Of the defenceless. Solitary ones
Hide from their robberies, for forth they go
Into the wilderness, their prey to hunt

Like ravening beasts.
There are, who watch to slay,
Rising before the dawn, or wrapp'd in night
Roaming with stealthy footstep, as a thief,
To smite their victims, while the wounded groan
Struck by their fatal shaft.
There are, who do
Such deeds of utter darkness as detest
The gaze of day. Muffling their face, they dig
Their way to habitations where they leave
Shame and dishonor.
Though He seem to sleep,
God's eye is on their ways. A little while
They wrap themselves in secret infamy,
Or proudly flourish,—but as the tall tree
Yields in a moment to the wrecking blast,
As 'neath the sickle falls the crisping corn,
Shall they be swept away, and leave no trace."

Bildad, the Shuhite, rose in act to speak.

"Dominion is with God, and fear. He makes
Peace in his own high places. Dost thou know
The number of His armies? Or on whom
His light ariseth not?
How then can man
Be justified with God? or he be pure
Born of a woman. Lo! the cloudless Moon,
And yon unsullied stars, are in His sight
Dim and impure. Can man who is a worm
Be spotless with his Maker?"

Hark, the voice
Of the afflicted man:
"How dost thou help
Him that is powerless? how sustain the arm
That fails in strength? how counsel him who needs
Wisdom? and how declare the righteous truth
Just as it is?
To Him who reads the soul,
Hades is naked, and the realms of Death
Have naught to cover them. This pendent Earth
Hangs on his word,—in gathering clouds he binds
The ponderous waters, till at his command
They rend their filmy prison. Day and night
Await his nod to run their measured course.
Heaven's pillars and its everlasting gates
Tremble at his reproof. The cleaving sea
And man's defeated pride confess his power.
Yet the same Hand that garnisheth the skies
Disdaineth not to fashion and sustain
The crooked serpent. But how small a part
Of all its works are understood by us
Dim dwellers in this lowly vestibule,
And by the thunders of mysterious power
Still held in awe.
As the Eternal lives
Who hath bow'd down my soul, as long as breath
Inspires this mortal frame, these lips shall ne'er
Utter deceit, nor cast away the wealth
Of a good conscience. While I live I'll hold

Fast mine integrity,—nor justify
The slanderous charges of a secret guilt
Ye bring against me.
For what is the gain
Of the base hypocrite when God shall take
Away his perjured soul? Yourselves have seen
How often in this life the wicked taste
Of retribution. The oppressor bears
Sway for a while,—but look!—the downfall comes.
His offspring shall not flourish, nor his grave
Be wet with widow's tears.
The unjust rich man
Heapeth up silver for a stranger's hand,
He hoardeth raiment with a miser's greed
To robe he knows not who, though he himself
Had grudg'd to wear it. Boastfully he builds
A costly mansion to preserve his name
Among the people. But like the slight booth,
Brief lodge of summer, shall it pass away.
Terrors without a cause, disable him
And drown his courage. Like a driven leaf
Before the whirlwind, shall he hasten down
To a dishonor'd tomb. Men shall rejoice,
And clap their hands, and hiss him from his place
When he departs.
Surely, there is a vein
For silver, and a secret bed for gold
Which man discovers. Where the iron sleeps
In darkest chambers of the mine he knows,

And how the brass is molten. But a Mind
Deeper than his, close-hidden things explores,
Searching out all perfection.
Earth unveils
The mystic treasures of her matron breast,
Bread for her children, gems like living flame,
Sapphires, whose azure emulates the skies,
And dust of gold. Yet there's a curtain'd path
Which the unfettered denizens of air
Have not descried, nor even the piercing eye
Of the black vulture seen. The lion's whelps
In their wide roaming, nor their fiercer sire
Have never trod it.
There's a Hand that bares
The roots of mountains at its will, and cuts
Through rifted rocks a channel, where the streams
And rivers freely flow—an Eye that scans
Each precious thing.
But where doth Wisdom dwell?
And in what curtain'd chamber was the birth
Of Understanding?
The great Sea uplifts
Its hand in adjuration, and declares
"*'Tis not with me*," and its unfathom'd deep
In subterranean thunders, echoing cry
"*No, not with me.*"
Offer ye not for them
Silver, or Ophir's gold, nor think to exchange
Onyx, or sapphire, or the coral branch

Or crystal gem where hides imprison'd light,
Nor make ye mention of the precious pearl
Or Ethiopian topaz, for their price
Transcendeth rubies, or the dazzling ray
Of concentrated jewels.
In what place
Are found these wondrous treasures? Who will show
Their habitation? which alike defies
The ken of those who soar, or those who delve
In cells profound.
Death and destruction say,
From their hoarse caverns, "We have heard their fame
But know them not."
Lo! He who weighs the winds
Measures the floods, controls the surging sea
And points the forked lightnings where to play,
He, unto whom all mysteries are plain
All secrets open, all disguises clear,
Saith unto man the questioner,—
"Behold
The fear of God is wisdom, and to break
The sway of evil and depart from sin
Is understanding."
Anguish wrings my soul
As in my hours of musing I restore
The picture of my lost prosperity,
When round my side my loving children drew
And from my happy home my steps were hail'd
Where'er I went. The fatherless and poor,

And he who had no helper, welcomed me
As one to right their wrongs, and pluck the spoil
From the oppressor's teeth. Pale widows raised
The glistening eye of gratitude, and they
Whose sight was quench'd, at my remembered tones
Pour'd blessings on me. Overflowing wealth
Brought me no titles that I held so dear
As father of the poor, and comforter
Of all who mourn.
When in the gate I sate
The nobles did me honor, and the wise
Sought counsel of me. To my words the young
Gave earnest heed, the white-hair'd men stood up,
And princes waited for my speech, as wait
The fields in summer for the latter rain.
But now, the children of base men spring up
And push away my feet, and make my name
A bye-word and a mockery, which was erst
Set to the harp in song.
Because my wealth
God hath resumed, they who ne'er dared to claim
Equality with even the lowest ones
Who watch'd my flock, they whom my menials scorned,
Dwellers in hovels, feeding like the brutes
On roots and bushes of the wilderness,
Despise me, and in mean derision cast
Marks of abhorrence at the fallen chief
Whom erst they fear'd.

Unpitied I endure
Sickness and pain that ope the narrow house
Where all the living go. My soul dissolves
And flows away as water—like the owl
In lone, forgotten cavern I complain,
For all my instruments of music yield
But mournful sounds, and from my organ comes
A sob of weeping.
I appeal to Him
Who sees my ways, and all my steps doth count,
If I have walk'd with vanity or worn
The veil of falsehood, or despised to obey
The law of duty; if I basely prowl'd
With evil purpose round my neighbor's door,
Or scorn'd my humblest menial's cause to right
When he contended with me, and complain'd,
Framed as he was of the same clay with me
By the same Hand Divine; or shunn'd to share
Even my last morsel with the hungry poor,
Or shield the uncovered suppliant with the fleece
Of my own cherish'd flock.
If ere I made
Fine gold my confidence, or lifted up
My heart in pride, because my wealth was great,
Or when I saw the glorious King of Day
Gladdening all nations, and the queenly Moon
Walking in brightness, was enticed to pay
A secret homage,—'twere idolatry
Unpardonably great.

If I rejoiced
In the affliction of mine enemy
Or for his hatred breathed a vengeful vow
When trouble came upon him,—if I closed
The inhospitable door against the foot
Of stranger, or of traveller,—or withheld
Full nutriment from any who abode
Within my tabernacle,—or refused
Due justice even to my own furrow'd field,
Then let my harvest unto thistles turn,
And rootless weeds o'ertop the beardless grain."

Then ceased the Man of Uz, like one o'erspent,
Feeling the fallacy of argument
With auditors like these, his thoughts withdrew
Into the shroud of silence, and he spake
No more unto them, standing fix'd and mute,
Like statued marble.
Then, as none replied,
A youthful stranger rose, and while he stretch'd
His hand in act to speak, and heavenward raised
His clear, unshrinking brow, he worthy seem'd
To hold the balance of that high debate.
Still, an indignant warmth, with energy
Of fervid eloquence his lips inspired.

—"I said that multitude of days should bring
Wisdom to man, and so gave earnest heed
To every argument. And lo! not one

Of all your speeches have convicted Job,
Or proved your theory that woes like his
Denote a secret guilt.
I listened still
With that respect which youth doth owe to age,
And till ye ceased to speak, refrain'd to show
Mine own opinion. But there is a breath
From the Almighty, that gives life to thought,
And in my soul imprison'd utterance burns
Like torturing flame. So, will I give it vent
Though I am young in years, and ye are old,
And should be wise. I will not shun to uphold
The righteous cause, nor will I gloze the wrong
With flattering titles, lest the kindling wrath
Of an offended Maker, sweep me hence.

Hearken, O Job, I pray thee, to my words
For they are words of truth.
Thou hast assumed
More perfect innocence than appertains
To erring man, and eager to refute
False accusation hast contemn'd the course
Of the All-Merciful.
Why shouldst thou strive
With Him whose might of wisdom ne'er unveils
Its mysteries to man? Yet doth He deign
Such hints and precepts as the docile heart
May comprehend. Sometimes in vision'd sleep,
His Spirit hovereth o'er the plastic mind

Sealing instruction. Or a different voice
Its sterner teaching tries. His vigor droops,
Strong pain amid the multitude of bones
Doth revel, till his soul abhorreth meat.
His fair flesh wastes, and downward to the pit
He hourly hastens. Holy Sympathy
May aid to uphold him in its blessed arms
Kindly interpreting the Will Divine,
With angel tenderness.
But if the God
Whose gracious ear doth hear the sigh of prayer
Baptized with dropping tears—perceives the cry
Of humbled self-abasing penitence,
He casts away the scourge—the end is gained.
Fresh as a child's, the wither'd flesh returns,
And life, and health, and joy, are his once more.
With discipline like this, He often tries
The creatures He hath made, to crush the seeds
Of pride, and teach that lowliness of soul
Befitting them, and pleasing in His sight.

Oh Man of Uz—if thou hast aught to add
Unto thy argument—I pray thee, speak!
Fain would I justify thee.
Is it well
To combat Him who hath the right to reign?
Or even to those who fill an earthly throne
And wear a princely diadem, to say,
Ye are unjust?

But how much less to Him
The fountain of all power, who heedeth not
Earth's vain distinctions, nor regards the rich
More than the poor, for all alike are dust
And ashes in His sight.

Is it not meet
For those who bear His discipline, to say
I bow submissive to the chastening Hand
That smites my inmost soul? Oh teach me that
Which through my blindness I have failed to see,
For I have sinn'd, but will offend no more.
Say, is it right, Oh Job, for thee to hold
Thyself superior to the All-Perfect Mind?
If thou art righteous what giv'st thou to Him
Who sits above the heavens? Can He receive
Favor from mortals?

Open not thy mouth
To multiply vain words, but rather bow
Unto the teaching of His works that spread
So silently around. His snows descend
And make the green Earth hoary. Chains of frost
Straighten her breadth of waters. Dropping rains
Refresh her summer thirst, or rending clouds
Roll in wild deluge o'er her. Roaming beasts
Cower in their dens affrighted, while she quakes
Convuls'd with inward agony, or reels
Dizzied with flashing fires.

Again she smiles
In her recovered beauty, at His will,

Maker of all things. So, He rules the world,
With wrath commingling mercy. Who may hope
With finite mind to understand His ways,
So excellent in power, in wisdom deep,
In justice terrible, respecting none
Who pride themselves in fancied wisdom."
Hark!
On the discursive speech a whirlwind breaks,
Tornadoes shake the desert, thunders roll
And from the lightning's startled shrine, *a voice!*
The voice of the Eternal.
"Who is this
That darkeneth knowledge by unmeaning words?
Gird up thy loins and answer.
Where wert thou
When the foundations of the earth were laid?
Who stretch'd the line, and fix'd the corner-stone,
When the bright morning-stars together sang
And all the hosts that circle round the Throne
Shouted for joy?
Whose hand controll'd the sea
When it brake forth to whelm the new-fram'd world?
Who made dark night its cradle and the cloud
Its swaddling-band? commanding
"Hitherto
Come, but no further. At this line of sand
Stay thy proud waves."
Hast thou call'd forth the morn
From the empurpled chambers of the east,

Or bade the trembling day-spring know its place?
Have Orion's depths been open'd to thy view?
And hast thou trod his secret floor? or seen
The gates of Death's dark shade?
Where doth light dwell?
And ancient Darkness, that with Chaos reign'd
Before Creation? Dost thou know the path
Unto their house, because thou then wert born?
And is the number of thy days so great?
Show me the treasure-house of snows. Unlock
The mighty magazines of hail, that wait
The war of elements.
Who hath decreed
A water-course for embryo fountain springs?
Mark'd out the lightning's path and bade the rain
O'erlook not in its ministries the waste
And desolate plain, but wake the tender herb
To cheer the bosom of the wilderness.
Tell me the father of the drops of dew,
The curdling ice, and hoary frost that seal
The waters like a stone, and change the deep
To adamant.
Bind if thou canst, the breath
And balmy influence of the Pleiades.
Bring forth Mazzaroth in his time, or guide
Arcturus, with his sons.
Canst thou annul
The fix'd decree that in their spheres detain
The constellations? Will the lightnings go

Forth on thine errands, and report to thee
As loyal vassals?
                                        Who in dying clay
Infused the immortal principle of mind,
And made them fellow-workers?
                                        If thou canst
Number the flying clouds, and gather back
Their falling showers, when parch'd and cleaving earth
Implores their charity. Wilt hunt the prey
With the stern forest-king? or dare invade
The darkened lair where his young lions couch
Ravenous with hunger?
                                        Who the ravens feeds
When from the parent's nest hurl'd out, they cry
And all forsaken, ask their meat from God?
Know'st thou the time when the wild goats endure
The mother-sorrow? how their offspring grow
Healthful and strong, uncared for, and unstall'd?
Who made the wild ass like the desert free,
Scorning the rein, and from the city's bound
Turning triumphant to the wilderness?
Lead to thy crib the unicorn, and bind
His unbow'd sinews to the furrowing plough,
And trust him if thou canst to bring thy seed
Home to the garner.
                                        Who the radiant plumes
Gave to the peacock? or the winged speed
That bears the headlong ostrich far beyond
The baffled steed and rider? not withheld

By the instinctive tenderness that chains
The brooding bird, she scatters on the sands
Her unborn hopes, regardless though the foot
May trampling crush them.
                                        Hast thou given the Horse
His glorious strength, and clothed his arching neck
With thunder? At the armed host he mocks,—
The rattling quiver, and the glittering spear.
Prancing and proud, he swalloweth the ground
With rage, and passionate desire to rush
Into the battle. At the trumpet's sound,
And shouting of the captains, he exults,
Drawing the stormy terror with delight
Into his fearless spirit.
                                        Doth the Hawk
In her migrations counsel ask of Thee?
Mounts the swift Eagle up at thy command?
Making her nest among the star-girt cliffs,
And thence undazzled by the vertic sun
Scanning the molehills of the earth, or motes
That o'er her bosom move.
                                        Say,—wilt thou teach
Creative Wisdom? or contend with Him
The Almighty,—ordering all things at His will?"

Then there was silence, till the chastened One
Murmured as from the dust,

"Lo, I am vile!
What shall I answer thee?—I lay my hand
Upon my mouth. Once have I dared to speak,
But would be silent now, forevermore."

—Yet still, in thunder, from the whirlwind's wing,
Jehovah's voice demanded,—
"Wilt thou dare
To disannul my judgments? and above
Unerring wisdom, and unbounded power
Exalt thine own?
Hast thou an arm like mine?
Array thyself in majesty, and look
On all the proud in heart, and bring them low,—
Yea, deck thyself with glory, cast abroad
The arrows of thine anger, and abase
The arrogant, and send the wicked down
To his own place, sealing his face like stone
Deep in the dust; for then will I confess
Thy might, and that thine own right hand hath power
To save thyself.
Hast seen my Behemoth,
Who on the grassy mountains finds his food?
And 'neath the willow boughs, and reeds, disports
His monstrous bulk?
His bones like brazen bars,
His iron sinews cased in fearful strength
Resist attack! Lo! when he slakes his thirst
The rivers dwindle, and he thinks to draw
The depths of Jordan dry.

Wilt cast thy hook
And take Leviathan? Wilt bind thy yoke
Upon him, as a vassal? Will he cringe
Unto thy maidens?

See the barbed spear
The dart and the habergeon, are his scorn.
Sling-stones are stubble, keenest arrows foil'd,
And from the plaited armor of his scales
The glittering sword recoils. Where he reclines,
Who is so daring as to rouse him up,
With his cold, stony heart, and breath of flame?
Or to the cavern of his gaping jaws
Thick set with teeth, draw near?

The Hand alone
That made him can subdue his baleful might."

Jehovah ceas'd,—for the Omniscient Eye
That scans the inmost thought of man, discern'd
Its work completed in that lowliness
Of deep humility which fits the soul
For heavenly intercourse, and renovates
The blessed image of obedient love
That Eden forfeited.

Out of the depths
Of true contrition sigh'd a trembling tone
In utter abnegation,

"I repent!
In dust and ashes. I abhor myself."

—Thus the returning prodigal who cries
Unclothed and empty, "Father! I have sinn'd,
And am not worthy to be called thy son,"
Finds full forgiveness, and a free embrace,
While the best robe his shrinking form enfolds.

But with this self-abasement toward his God
Job mingled tenderest regard for man.
No longer with indignant warmth he strove
Against his false accusers, or retained
Rankling remembrance of the enmity
That vexed his wounded soul
With earnest prayers
And offerings, he implored offended Heaven
To grant forgiveness to those erring friends,
Paying with love the alienated course
Of their misguided minds.
Heaven heard his voice,
And with that intercession sweet, return'd
The sunbeams of his lost prosperity.
Back came his buried joys. They had no power
To harm a soul subdued. The refluent tide
Of wealth swept o'er him. On his many hills
Gathered the herds, and o'er his pastures green
Sported the playful lambs. The tuneful voice
Of children fill'd his desolate home with joy,
And round his household board their beauty gleam'd,
Making his spirit glad.

So full of days,
While twice our span of threescore years and ten,
Mark'd out its silvery chronicle of moons
Still to his knee his children's children climb'd
To hear the wisdom he had learned of God
Through the strong teaching both of joy and woe.

Nor had this sublunary scene alone,
Witness'd his trial. Doubt ye not that forms
To earth invisible were hovering near
With the sublime solicitude of Heaven.
For he, the bold, bad Spirit, in his vaunting pride
Of impious revolt, had dared to say
Unto the King of Kings,
"Stretch forth thy hand
And take away all that he hath, and Job
Will curse Thee to Thy face."
Methinks we hear
An echo of angelic harmony
From that blest choir who struck their harps with joy
That from the Tempter's ordeal he had risen
An unhurt victor. Round the Throne they pour'd
Their gratulations that the born of clay
Tho' by that mystery bow'd which ever veils
The inscrutable counsels of the All-Perfect One,
Might with the chieftain of the Rebel Host
Cope unsubdued and heavenward hold his way.

THE RURAL LIFE IN NEW-ENGLAND.

INTRODUCTION.

It may be thought that the following poem, especially its opening Canto is too minute and circumstantial in its descriptions. Yet the habitudes of a past and peculiar generation, fast fading from remembrance, are worthy of being preserved, though little accordant with romance, perhaps with poetry. So rapid has been our progress as a people, that dimness gathers over the lineaments of even our immediate ancestry. Yet traits at one period despised, or counted obsolete, may at another be diligently sought after and re-juvenated.

It has been observed that nations reaching their zenith, regard with more complacency their rising morn, than the approaching west. France, notwithstanding the precision given to her language by Richilieu, and the Academy, turns back affectionately to her Troubadours and Trouvires, to the long-drawn, scarce-readable "Romance of the Rose," and the itinerant Chronicles of Froissart. England is not indifferent to Anglo-Saxon traditions, or the customs of her Norman dynasty.

A time may arrive when our posterity will not scorn to be reminded of the primitive usages of their rural fathers. To that time, and to unborn readers, this simple poem is dedicated.

L. H. S.

THE RURAL LIFE IN NEW-ENGLAND.

CANTO FIRST.

PEACEFUL is the rural life, made strong by healthful industry,
Firm in love of the birth-land, and the laws that govern it,
Calm through moderated desires and a primitive simplicity,
Walking filially with Nature as the Patriarchs walked with God.
Such have I beheld it in my native vales, green and elm-shaded.
Such hath it been depicted in their legends who went before me;
What therefore, I have seen and heard, declare I unto you
In measures artless and untuneful.
Fearless of hardship,
In costume, as in manners, unadorn'd and homely
Were our ancestral farmers, the seed-planters of a strong nation.
Congenial were their wives, not ashamed of the household charge,
Yoke-fellows that were help-meets, vigorous and of a good courage;

Revolting not at life's plain intent, but its duties discharging
Patiently, lovingly, and with true faith looking upward.
Thence came the rudiments of an inflexible people
Whose praise is in themselves.
Hail to the ancient farmer!
Broad-shouldered as Ajax—deep-chested through commerce with free air,
Not enervated by luxury, nor care-worn with gold-counting,
Content with his lot, by pride and envy unvisited.
Muscular was his arm, laying low the kings of the forest,
Uncouth might be his coat, and his heavy shoes, Vestris flouted,
At the grasp of his huge hand, the dainty belle might have shuddered.
Yet blessings on his bronzed face, and his warm, honest heart,
Whose well-rooted virtues were the strength and stay of republics.

True independence was his, earth and sky being his bankers,
Bills drawn on them, endorsed by toil were never protested.
Bathed in vernal dews was his glistening plough-share,
Birds, newly-returned, the merry nest-builders, bade him good morrow,
Keenly wrought his scythe in summer, where fell the odorous clover,
Clear was his song at autumn-husking, amid piles of golden corn.
Winter saw him battling the drifted snows, with his oxen,

Bearing to the neighboring town, fuel that gladden'd the
hearth-stone.
Deep in undisturbed beds then slept the dark-featured anthracite,
Steam not having armed itself to exterminate the groves,
Lavishly offering them as a holocaust to winged horses of
iron,
Like Moloch, cruel god, dooming the beautiful to the flame.

Independent was the farmer, the food of his household
being sure;
With the fields of waving grain; with the towering tassell'd
maize;
With the herds, moving homeward, bearing their creamy
nectar;
He saw, and gather'd it, giving thanks to the bountiful
Father.
Among the lambs sporting in green pastures, among the
feathery people,
Among the fruit-laden branches, he beheld it also;
Under the earth, on the earth, in the air, ripen'd his threefold crop.
Swelling in the cluster'd vine, and the roots of the teeming
garden,
The Garden—precious spot! which God deign'd to bless at
the beginning,
Placing therein Man, made after his own glorious image,
To dress it and to keep it.

Hail, to the ancient farmer,
Naught to him the fall of stocks that turns pale the speculator,
Naught to him the changes of trade, wrinkling the brow of the merchant,
Naught to him, the light weight, or exorbitant price of the baker;
Sure was his bread, howsoe'er the markets might fluctuate,
Sweet loaves of a rich brown, plentifully graced his table,
Made by the neat hand of wife or daughter, happy in healthful toil.
Skilfully wrought the same hands, amid the treasures of the dairy,
Rich cheeses, and masses of golden butter, and bowls of fragrant milk
Not doled out warily, as by city dames, but to all, free and flowing;
Woman's right it was, to crown the board with gifts of her own preparing;
Rights not disputed, not clamored for in public assemblies,
But conceded by approving Love, whose manliness threw around her
A cherishing protection, such as God willed in Paradise.

Dense was the head of the Maple, and in summer of a lustrous green,
Yet earliest in autumn, among all trees of the forest,
To robe itself in scarlet, like a cardinal going to conclave.
Subjected was it in spring, to a singular phlebetomy;

Tubes inserted through its bark, drew away the heart's sweet
blood,
Pore after pore emptying itself, till the great arteries were
exhausted.
Fires then blazed amid the thickets, like the moveable camp
of the gipsies,
And in boiling kettles, fiercely eddying, struggled the caloric,
With gases, and the saccharine spirit, until the granulated
sugar,
Showed a calm, brown face, welcome to the stores of the
housewife;
Moulded also into small cakes, it formed the favorite confec-
tion
Of maiden and swain, during the long evenings of courtship.

Gamboling among wild flowers, gadded the honey-bee,
Bending down their innocent heads, with a buzzing lore of
flattery,
Beguiling them of their essences, which with tireless alacrity,
Straightway deposited he in his cone-roof'd banking-house,
Subtle financier—thinking to take both dividend and capital.
But failing in his usury, for duly cometh the farmer,
Despoiling him of his hoard, yea! haply of his life also.
Stern was the policy of the olden times, to that diligent in-
sect,
Not skill'd like our own, to confiscate a portion of his earn-
ings,
Leaving life and limb unscathed for future enterprise.

Welcome were the gifts of that winged chemist to a primitive people.
Carefully cloistered in choice vases, was the pure, virgin honey,
Sacred to honor'd guests, or a balm to the sore-throated invalid.
Dealt out charily, was the fair comb to the gratified little ones,
Or, to fermentation yielded, producing the spirited metheglin.
Not scorn'd by the bee-masters, were even those darken'd hexagons
Where slumber'd the dead like the coral-builders in reefy cell.
Even these to a practical use devoted the clear-sighted matron,
Calling forth from cavernous sepulchres cheerful light for the living.
Cleansed and judiciously mingled with an oleagenous element,
Thus drew she from the mould, waxen candles, whose gold-tinted beauty
Crown'd proudly the mantel-piece, reserved for bettermost occasions.
Unheard of, then, was the gas, with briliant jet and gorgeous chandelier,
Nor hunted they from zone to zone, with barbed harpoon the mighty whale,
Making the indignant monarch of ocean, their flambeau and link-boy:

For each household held within itself, its own fountain of light.
Faithful was the rural housewife, taking charge of all intrusted things,
Prolonging the existence of whatever needed repair,
Requiring children to respect the property of their parents,
Not to waste or destroy, but be grateful for food and clothing;
Teaching them industry, and the serious value of fleeting time,
Strict account of which must be rendered to the Master and Giver of Life.
Prudence was then held in esteem and a laudable economy
Not jeered at by miserly names, but held becoming in all,
For the poor, that they might avoid debt; and the rich that they might be justly generous.

Ho! for the flax-field, with its flower of blue and leaf freshly green,—
Ho! for the snowy fleece, which the quiet flock yield to their master,—
Woman's hand shall transmute both, into armor for those she loves,
Wrapping her household in comfort, and her own heart in calm content.
Hark! at her flaxen distaff cheerily singeth the matron,
Hymns, that perchance, were mingled with her own cradle melodies.

Back and forth, at the Great Wheel, treadeth the buxom
damsel,
Best form of calisthenics, exercising well every muscle
Regularly and to good purpose, filling the blue veins with
richer blood.
Rapidly on the spindle, gather threads from the pendent roll,
Not by machinery anatomized, till stamina and staple fly
away,
But with hand-cards concocted, and symmetrically formed,
Of wool, white or grey, or the refuse flax smoothed to a
silky lustre,
It greeteth the fingers of the spinner.
In this Hygeian concert
Leader of the Orchestra, was the Great Wheel's tireless
tenor,
Drowning the counter of the snapping reel, and the quill-
wheels fitful symphony,
Whose whirring strings, yielded to children's hands, prepare
spools for the shuttle.
At intervals, like a muffled drum, sounded the stroke of the
loam,
Cumbrous, and filling a large space, with its quantity of
timber,
Obedient only to a vigorous arm, which in ruling it grew
more vigorous.
From its massy beam were unrolled, fabrics varied and
substantial,
Linen for couch and table, and the lighter garniture of
summer,

Frocks of a flaxen color for the laborer, or striped with blue for the younglings;
Stout garments in which man bides the buffet of wintry elements..
From the rind of the stately butternut, drew they a brown complexion,
Or the cerulean borrowed from the tint of the southern indigo.
Thus rustic Industry girded itself, amid household music,
As History of old, set her fabulous legends to the harp.
Ears trained to the operas of Italy, would find discordance to be mocked at,
But the patriot heard the ring of gold in the coffers of his country,
Not sent forth to bankruptcy, for the flowery silks of France;
While the listening christian caught the strong harmonies of a peaceful Land,
Giving praise to Jehovah.
Lo! at the winter evening
In these uncarpeted dwellings, what a world of comfort!
Large hickory logs send a dancing flame up the ample chimney,
Tinging with ruddy gleam, every face around the broad hearth-stone.
King and patriarch, in the midst, sitteth the true-hearted farmer.
At his side, the wife with her needle, still quietly regardeth the children.

Sheltered in her corner-nook, in the arm-chair, the post of honor,
Calm with the beauty of age, is the venerable grandmother.
Clustering around her, watching the stocking that she knits, are the little ones,
Loving the stories that she tells of the days when she was a maiden,
Stories ever mix'd with lessons of a reverent piety.
Manna do they thus gather to feed on, when their hair is hoary.
Stretch'd before the fire, is the weary, rough-coated house-dog,
Winking his eyes, full of sleep, at the baby, seated on his shoulder,
Proudly watching his master's darling, and the pet of the family,
As hither and thither on its small feet it toddles unsteadily.

On the straight-back'd oaken settle, congregate the older children.
Work have they, or books, and sometimes the weekly news-paper,
Grey, on coarse, crumpled paper, and borrowed from house to house,
Small-sized, yet precious, and read through from beginning to end,
Bright, young heads circling close, peering together over its columns.
Now and then, furtive glances reconnoitre the ingle-side,

Where before a bed of coals, rows of red apples are roasting,
Spitting out their life-juices spitefully, in unwilling martyrdom.
Finished, and drawn back, the happy group wait a brief interval,
Thinking some neighbor might chance to come in and bid them good even,
Heightening their simple refection, for whose sake would be joyously added
The mug of sparkling cider passed temperately from lip to lip,
Sufficient and accepted offering of ancient, true-hearted hospitality.
Thus in colonial times dwelt they together as brethren,
Taking part in each others' concerns with an undissembled sympathy.

But when the tall old clock told out boldly three times three,
Thrice the number of the graces, thrice the number of the fates,
The full number of the Muses, the hour dedicated to Morpheus,
At that curfew departed the guest, and all work being suspended,
Laid aside was the grandmother's knitting-bag, for in its cradle
Rock'd now and then by her foot, already slumbered the baby.
Then, ere the fading brands were covered with protecting ashes,

Rose the prayer of the Sire, amid his treasured and trusted ones,
Rose his thanks for past blessings, his petitions for the future,
His committal of all care to Him who careth for his creatures,
Overlooking nothing that His bountiful Hand hath created.

Orderly were the households of the farmer, not given to idle merriment,
Honoring the presence of parents, as of tutelary spirits.
To be obedient and useful were the first lessons of the young children,
Well learned and bringing happiness, that ruled on sure foundations,
Respect for authority, being the initial of God's holy fear.
Modern times might denounce such a system as tyrannical,
Asking the blandishments of indulgence, and a broader liberty;
Leaving in perplexing doubt, the mind of the infant stranger
Whether to rule or to be ruled he came hither on his untried journey,
Rearing him in headstrong ignorance, revolting at discipline,
Heady, high-minded, and prone to speak evil of dignities.

Welcome was Winter, to the agriculturist of olden times,
Then, while fruitful Earth, with whom he was in league, held her sabbath,
Knowledge entered into his soul. At the lengthened evening,
Read he in an audible voice to his listening family
Grave books of History, or elaborate Theology,
Taxing thought and memory, but not setting fancy on tiptoe

Teaching reverence for wise men, and for God, the Giver of Wisdom.
Not then had the era arrived, when of making books there is no end.
Painfully the laboring press, brought forth like the kingly whale
One cub at a time, guiding it carefully over the billows,
Watching with pride and pleasure, its own wonderful offspring.
A large, fair volume, was in those days, as molten gold,
Touched only with clean hands, and by testators willed to their heirs.

Winter also, brought the school for the boys,—released from farm-labor.
Early was the substantial breakfast, in those short, frosty mornings,
That equipped in season, might be the caravan for its enterprise,
Punctuality in those simple times being enrolled among the virtues.
There they go! a rosy group, bearing in small baskets their dinner;
Plunging thro' all snow-drifts, the boys,—on all ices sliding the girls,
Yet leaving not the straight path, lest tardy should be their arrival.
Lone on the bleak hill-side, stood the unpainted village school-house,

Winds taking aim at it like a target, smoke belching from its chimney,
Bare to the fiery suns of summer, like the treeless Nantucket.
Desks were ranged under the windows where on high benches without backs
Sate the little ones, their feet vainly reaching toward the distant floor,
Commanded everlastingly to keep still and to be still,
As if immobility were the climax of all excellence;
Hard lesson for quick nerves, and eyes searching for something new.
Nature endowed them with curiosity, but man wiser than she
Calling himself a teacher, would fain stiffen them into statues.
No bright visions of the school-palaces of future days
With seats of ease, and carpets, and pianos, and pictured walls,
And green lawns, pleasantly shaded, stretching wide for play,
And knowledge fondling her pets, and unveiling her royal road,
Gleam'd before them as Eden, kindling smiles on their thoughtful faces.

Favor'd were the elder scholars with more congenial tasks:
Loudly read they in their classes, glorying in the noise they made,
Busily over the slates moved the hard pencils, with a grating sound,

Diligently on coarse paper wrote they, with quill pens, bushy topp'd,
Blessed in having lived, ere the metallic stylus was invented.
Rang'd early around the fire, have been their frozen ink-stands,
Where in rotation sits each scholar briefly, by the master's leave,
Roasting on one side, and on the other a petrefaction,
Keen blasts through the crevices delighting to whistle and mock them.
Patient were the children, not given to murmuring or complaining,
Learning through privation, lessons of value for a future life,
Subjection, application, and love of knowledge for itself alone.
On a high chair, sate the solemn Master, watchful of all things,
Absolute was his sway and in this authority he gloried,
Conforming it much to the Spartan rule, and the code of Solomon,
Showing no mercy to idleness, or wrong uses of the slippery tongue:
Yet to diligent students kind, and of their proficiency boastful,
Exhibiting their copy-books, to committee-man and visitant,
Or calling out the declaimers, in some stentorian dialogue.
Few were the studies then pursued, but thoroughness required in all,

Surface-work not being in vogue, nor rootless blossoms regarded.
Especially well-taught was the orthography of our copious language,
False spelling being as a sin to be punished by the judges.
In this difficult attainment the master sometimes accorded
A form of friendly conflict sought with ardor as a premium,
Stirring the belligerent element, ever strong in boyish natures.
Forth came at close of the school-day, two of reproachless conduct,
Naming first the best spellers, they proceeded to choose alternately,
Till all, old and young, ranging under opposite banners,
Drawn up as in battle array, each other stoutly confronted.
Rapidly given out by the leaders to their marshall'd forces,
Word by word, with its definition, was the allotted lesson,
Vociferously answered from each side like discharges of artillery;
Fatal was the slightest mistake, fatal even pause or hesitation,
Doubt was for the vanquished, to deliberate was to be lost.
Drooping with disgrace down sate each discomfited pupil,
Bravely stood the perfect, the most unbroken line gaining the victory.
Not unboastful were the conquerers, cheered with shouts on their homeward way,
Crest-fallen were the defeated, yet eager for a future contest.
Strong elements thus enlisted, gave new vigor to mental toil,

As the swimmer puts forth more force till the rapids are overpast.
Dear to the persevering, were those schools of the olden time,
Respected were the teachers, who with majestic austerity,
Dispensed without favoritism, a Lacedamonian justice.
Learning was not then loved for luxury, like a lady for her gold,
But testing her worshippers by trial, knew who sought her for herself.

Not given to frequent feasting was the home-bred farmer of New England,
Parties, and the popular lectures swelled not his code of enjoyments.
One banquet, climax of his convivial delight, was the yearly thanksgiving,
Substituted by puritan settlers for the Christmas of the Mother-Clime,
Keeping in memory the feast of ingathering, of the Ancient Covenant People;
Drear November was its appointed season, when earth's bounty being garnered,
Man might rest from his labors, and praise the Lord of the Harvest.
Such was its original design, but the tendencies of Saxonism,
Turn'd it more to eating and drinking, than devotional remembrance.
Yet blessed was the time, summoning homeward every wanderer:

Back came the city apprentice, and from her service place the damsel,
Back came the married daughter to the father's quiet hearthstone,
Wrapped warmly in her cloak is a babe, its eyes full of wonder,—
Hand in hand, walked the little ones, bowing low before the grandparents,
Meekly craving their blessing, for so had they been piously taught.
Back to the birth-spot, to the shadow of their trees ancestral,
Came they like joyous streams, to their first untroubled fountain,
Knowing better how to prize it, from the rocks that had barred their course.
In primitive guise, journeyed homeward those dispersed ones.
Rare, in these days, was the carriage, or stage-coach for the traveller;
Roads, unmacadamized, making rude havoc of delicate springs.
Around the door, horses gather with the antique side-saddle and pillion,
Led thence to the full barn, while their riders find heartfelt welcome.

Then all whom culinary cares release, hasten to the House of Worship,
Religion being invoked to sanction the rejoicing of the fathers.

Plain was the village-church, a structure of darkened wood,
Having doors on three sides, and flanked by sheds for the horses,
Guiltless of blackening stove-pipe, or the smouldering fires of the furnace.
Assaulted oft were its windows, by the sonorous North-Western,
Making organ-pipes in the forest, for its shrill improvisations
Patient of cold, sate the people, each household in its own square pew,
Palisaded above the heads of the children, imprisoning their roving eyes.
Patiently sate the people, while from 'neath the great sounding-board,
The preacher unfolded his sermon, like the many-headed cauliflower.
Grave was the good pastor, not prone to pamper animal appetites,
But mainly intent to deal with that which is immortal.
Prolix might he have been deemed, save by the flock he guided,
Who duteously accounted him but a little lower than the angels.

As solemn music to the sound of his monotonous periods
Listened attentively the young, until he slowly enunciated
Fifteenthly, in the division of his elaborate discourse.
Then gadded away their busy thoughts to the Thanksgiving dinner,
Visioning good things to come.

At length, around the table,
Duly bless'd by the Master of the feast, they cheerily assemble.
Before him, as his perquisite, and prerogative to carve.
In a lordly dish smokes the huge, well-browned Turkey,
Chickens were there, to whose innocent lives Thanksgiving is ever a death-knell;
Luscious roasters from the pen, the large ham of a red complexion,
Garnish'd and intermingled with varied forms of vegetable wealth.
Ample pasties were attached, and demolished with dexterity,
Custards and tarts, and compounds of the golden-faced pumpkin,
Prime favorite, without whose aid, scarcely could New England have been thankful.
Apples, with plump, waxen cheeks, chestnuts, and the fruit of the hickory,
Bisected neatly, without fragment, furnished the simple dessert,
Finale to that festival where each guest might be safely merry.
Hence, by happy-hearted children, was it hailed as the pole-star,
Toward which Memory looked backward six months, and Hope forward for six to come,
Dating reverently from its era, as the Moslem from his Hegira.

Hymen also hailed it as his revenue, and crowning time;
Bachelors wearied with the restraints that courtship imposes,
Longed for it, as the Israelite for the jubilee of release,
And many a householder, in his family-bible marked its date
As the day of his espousals, and of the gladness of his heart.

Content was the life of agriculture, in unison with that wisest prayer
" *Thy will be done.*" Wisest, because who, save the Eternal
Knoweth what is best for man, walking ignorantly among shadows,
Himself a shadow, not like Adam our father in Paradise,
Rightly naming all things, but calling evil, good, and good, evil,
Blindly blaming the discipline that might bless him everlastingly,
And embracing desires, that in their bosom hide the dagger of Ehud.
Asketh he for honor? In its train are envyings and cares;
Wealth? It may drown the soul in destruction and perdition;
Power? Lo! it casteth on some lone St. Helena to die:
Surely, safest of all petitions, is that of our blessed Saviour,—
"*Not my will but Thine.*"

Thus, as it was in the days before us,
Rural life in New-England, with its thrift, and simplicity,

Minutely have I depicted, not emulous of embellishment.
More of refinement might it boast when our beautiful birth-clime,
From the colonial chrysalis emerging, spread her wing among the nations.
Then rose an aristocracy, founded not on wealth alone
That winds may scatter like desert sands, or the floods wash away,
But on the rock of solid virtue, where securely anchors the soul.

Mid its cultured acres rose gracefully a dwelling of the better class,
Large, but not lofty, its white walls softened by surrounding shades,
Fresh turf at its feet like velvet, green boughs bannering its head,
Bannering, and dropping music, till the last rustle of the falling leaves.
There, still in her comely prime, dwelt the lady of the mansion.
Moderate would her fortune be held in these days that count by millions,
Yet rich was she, because having no debts, what seemed to be hers, was so;
Rich, in having a surplus for the poor, which she gladly imparted;
Rich too, through Agriculture, pursued less from need than habit.

Habit mingled with satisfaction, and bringing health in its train.
Early widowhood had touched her brow with sadness such as time bringeth,
Yet in her clear eye was a fortitude, surmounting adversity.
Busy were her maidens, and happy, their right conduct kindly approved,
Busy also the swains thro' whose toil her fields yielded increase,
Respect had she for labor; knowing both what to require, and when it was well performed,
Readily rendering full wages, with smiles and words of counsel,
Accounting those who served her, friends, entitled to advice and sympathy.
Thus, looking well to the ways of her household, and from each expecting their duty,
Wisely divided she her time, and at intervals of leisure,
Books allured her cultured mind through realms of thought and knowledge.

But the deepest well-spring of her joys, not yet hath been unfolded,
A fountain where care and sorrow forgot both their name and nature.
Two little daughters, like olive plants, grew beside that fountain,
One, with dark, deepset eyes, and wealth of raven tresses,
The other gleaming as a sunbeam, through her veil of golden hair,

With a glance like living sapphire, making the beholder glad.
Clinging to the sweet mother's hand, smiling when she smiled,
If she were sad, grieving also, they were her blessed comforters,
Morn and Even were they styled by admiring, fanciful visitants,
So "the evening and the morning, were to her soul the first day,"
After the heavy midnight of her weeping and widowhood.

Side by side, in sweet liberty hither and thither roamed those little ones,
Hunting violets on the bank, tasting cheese curds in the dairy,
Seeking red and white strawberries, as ripening they ran in the garden beds,
To fill the small basket for their mother, covering the fruit with rose-buds,
Peering archly to see if she would discover what was lurking beneath.
Gamboling with the lambs, shouting as the nest-builders darted by,
Sharing in the innocence of one, and catching song from the other.

Nightly on the same snowy pillow, were laid their beautiful heads,
The same morning beam kiss'd away their lingering slumbers,

The first object that met their waking eye, was the bright, sisterly smile.
One impulse moved both hearts, as kneeling by their little bed,
Breathed forth from ruby lips, "Our Father, who art in Heaven!"
Simple homage, meekly blending in a blessed stream of incense.

Forth went they among the wild flowers, making friendship with the dragon-fly,
With the ant in her circling citadel, with the spider at her silk-loom,
Talking to the babbling brook, speaking kindly to the uncouth terrapin,
And frog, who to them seem'd dancing joyously in watery halls.
Like the chirping of the wood-robin murmured their tuneful voices,
Or rang out in merry laughter, gladdening the ear of the Mother,
Who when she heard it afar off, laughed also, not knowing wherefore.

Thus, in companionship with Nature, dwelt they, growing each day more happy,
Loving all things that she cherish'd, and loved by her in return.
Yet not idly pass'd their childhood, in New England's creed that were heresy,

Promptly, as strength permitted, followed they examples of industry,
Lovingly assisting the Mother wherever her work might be.
Surprising was it to see what their small hands could accomplish,
Without trespassing on the joy of childhood, that precious birthright of life.
Diligently wrought they in summer, at the dame's school with plodding needle,
Docile at their lessons in winter, stood they before the Master:
Yet learning most from Home and Mother, those schools for the heart,
Befitting best that sex, whose sphere of action is in the heart.
Attentive were they to the Parents' rule, and to the open book of Nature,
Teachers, whose faithful pupils shall be wise towards God.

Different were the two daughters, though to the same discipline subjected.
Grave was the elder born and thoughtful, even beyond her years,
Night upon her tresses, but the star of morning in her heart.
Exceeding fair was the younger, and witty, and full of grace,
Winning with her sunny ringlets, the notice of all beholders.
Different also were their temperaments, one loving like the Violet
Shaded turf, where the light falls subdued through sheltering branches,

The other, as the Tulip, exulting in the lustrous noontide,
And the prerogatives of beauty, to see, and to be seen.
Sweet was it to behold them, when the sun grew low in summer,
Riding gracefully through the green-wood, each on her ambling palfrey,
One, white as milk, and the other like shining ebony,
For so in fanciful love had the Mother selected for her darlings.
Sweet was it to mark them, side by side, in careless beauty,
Looking earnestly in each others' faces, thought playfully touching thought.

Chief speaker was Miranda, ever fearless and most fluent.
"Tired am I of always seeing the same dull, old scenes.
I wish the rail-fences would tumble down, and the sprawling apple-trees,—
And the brown farm-houses take unto themselves wings and fly away,
Like the wild-geese in autumn, if only something might be new.
There's the Miller forever standing on that one same spot of ground,
Watching his spouting wheel, when there's water, and when there is none,
Grumbling, I suppose, at home, to his spiritless wife and daughters.
I like not that fusty old Miller, his coat covered with meal,
Ever tugging at bags, and shoveling corn into the hopper."

Discreetly answer'd Bertha, and the lively one responded,
Lively, and quick-sighted, yet prone to be restless and unsatisfied,
"Counting rain-drops as they fall, one by one, from sullen branches.
Seeing silly lambkins leap, and the fan-tail'd squirrels scamper,
What are such things to me? Stupid Agriculture I like not,
Soap-making, and the science of cheese-tubs, what are they to me?
The chief end of life with these hinds and hindesses,
Is methinks, to belabor their hands, till they harden like brick-bats."

"Look, look, Miranda, dearest! The new moon sweetly rising
Holdeth forth her silver crescent, which the loyal stars perceiving,
Gather gladly to her banner, like a host around their sovereign.
Let us find the constellations that our good Instructor taught us.
Remember you not yesterday, when our lesson was well-render'd,
How with unwonted flattery he call'd us his Hesperus and Aurora?"

"These hum-drum teachings tire me, I'm disgusted with reciting

And repeating, day by day, what I knew well enough
before."
Then quickening briskly her startled steed with the riding-
whip,
She darted onward through the forest, reaching first their
own abode.

At night, when they retired, ere the waning lamp was
extinguished,
That good time for talking, when heart to heart discloseth
What the work or the pride of day, might in secrecy have
shrouded,
Said Miranda,
"I have seen our early play-mate, Emilia,
From a boarding-school return'd, all accomplished, all de-
lightful,
So changed, so improved, her best friends might scarcely
know her.
Why might not I be favor'd with similar advantages?
Caged here, year by year, with wings beating the prison-
door;
I would fain go where she went. If overruled I shall be
wretched.
I *must* go, Bertha, yes! No obstacle shall withhold me."

"Oh Miranda! Our Mother! In your company is her
solace.
In your young life she liveth, at your bright smile, ever
smileth,

Such power have you to cheer her. What could she do without you
When the lengthen'd eve grows lonely, and the widow sorrow presseth ? "
" Oh persuade her ! " she cried, with an embrace of passionate fervor,
" Persuade her, Bertha ! and I'll be your bond-servant forever."

Seldom had a differing purpose ruffled long those sisterly bosoms.
Wakeful lay Bertha, the silent tear for her companion,
While frequent sighs swelling and heaving the snowy breast of Miranda,
Betray'd that troubled visions held her spirit in their custody.

Like twin streamlets had they been, from one quiet fountain flowing,
Stealing on through fringed margins, anon playfully diverging,
Yet to each other as they wander'd, sending messages through whispering reeds,
Then returning and entwining joyously, with their cool chrystalline arms.

But who that from their source marketh infant brooklets issue,

Like sparkling threads of silver, wending onward through the distance
Can foretell which will hold placid course among the vallies,
Content with silent blessings from the fertile soil it cheereth,
Or which, mid rocky channels contending and complaining,
Now exulting in brief victory, then in darken'd eddies creeping,
Leaps its rampart and is broken on the wheel of the cataract.

Generous is the love and holy that springeth from gratitude;
Rooting not in blind instinct, grasping not, exacting not,
Remembering the harvest on which it fed, and the toil of the harvester;
Fain would it render recompense according to what it hath received,
Or falling short, weepeth. As the leaf of the white Lily
Bendeth backward to the stalk whence its young bud drew nutrition,
So turneth the Love of Gratitude, with eye undimm'd and fervent,
To parent, friend, teacher, benefactor, bountiful Creator.
Sympathies derived from such sources ever sacredly cherishing;
Daughter of Memory, inheriting her mother's immortality,
Welcome shall she find among angels, where selfish love may not enter.

CANTO SECOND.

In the gay and crowded city
Where the tall and jostling roof-trees
Jealous seem of one another,
Jealous of the ground they stand on,
Each one thrusting out its neighbor
From the sunrise, or the sunset,
In a boarding school of fashion
Was Miranda comprehended,
Goal of her supreme ambition.

—Girls were there from different regions,
Distant States, and varying costumes,
She was beautiful they told her,
And her mirror when she sought it
Gave concurrent testimony.

—Many teachers met their classes
In this favorite Institution
Where accomplishments or studies
Were pursued as each selected,
Or their parents gave commandment.
But Miranda was impeded

In successful application,
By the consciousness of beauty
And the vanity it fosters.

—Very fond was she of walking
In the most frequented places,
Fondly fancying all beholders
Gazed on her with admiration.
Striking dresses, gay with colors
She disported and commended,
Not considering that the highest
Of attractions in a woman
Is simplicity of costume,
And a self-forgetful sweetness.

—Men with business over-laden,
Men of science, pondering axioms,
Men of letters, lost in reverie,
She imagined when they passed her
Gaz'd with secret admiration,
Ask'd in wonder, "*who can that be?*"
Backward turned perchance, to view her,
As she lightly glided onward.

—So completely had this beauty
Leagued with vanity, uprooted
Serious thought and useful purpose,
And the nobler ends of being,
That even in the solemn Temple
Where humility befitteth

All who offer adoration,
Close observance of the apparel
Of acquaintances or strangers,
And a self-display intruded
On the service of devotion,
While her fair cheek oft-times rested
Daintily on gloveless fingers
Where the radiant jewels sparkled
On a hand like sculptured marble.

Meantime in the rural mansion
Whence with gladness she departed,
Sate the mother and the sister
By the hearth-stone or the lamp-light,
Thinking of their loved Miranda,
Speaking of her, working for her,
Writing tender, earnest letters
To sustain her mid her studies,
Fearing that her health might suffer
By the labor and privation
That a year at school demanded.

—As the autumnal evenings lengthen'd,
Bertha with a filial sweetness
Sought her mother's favorite authors,
And with perfect elocution
Made their sentiments and feelings,
Guests around the quiet fireside.

—Page of Livy, or of Cæsar,
Stirring scenes of tuneful Maro,

From their native, stately numbers
To the mother's ear she rendered;
Or with her o'er ancient regions,
Fallen sphynx, or ruin'd column,
Led by guiding Rollin, wandered,
Deeply mused with saintly Sherlock,
Or through Milton's inspiration
Scanned the lore of forfeit Eden.

With the vertic rays of Summer
Homeward came the fair Miranda.
How the village people wonder'd
At her fashions, and her movements,
How she made the new piano
Tremble to its inmost centre
With *andante*, and *bravura*,
What a piece she had to show them
Of Andromache the Trojan,
Wrought in silks of every color,
And 'twas said a foreign language
Such as princes use in Paris,
She could speak to admiration.

—Greatly their surprise amused her,
But the Mother and the Sister
With their eagle-eyed affection,
Spied a thorn amid the garland,
Heard the sighing on her pillow,
Saw the flush invade her forehead,

And were sure some secret sorrow
Rankled in that snowy bosom.

Rumor, soon with hundred voices
Whisper'd of a dashing lover,
Irreligious and immoral,
And the anxious Mother counsel'd
Sad of heart her fair-hair'd daughter.

—Scarce with any show of reverence
Listen'd the impatient maiden,
Then with tearless eyes wide open
Like full orbs of shadeless sapphire
All unpausing, thus responded.

—"I have promised Aldebaran,
To be his,—alone,—forever!
And I'll keep that promise, Mother,
Though the firm skies fall around me,
And yon stars in fragments shatter'd,
Each with thousand voices warn'd me.

—Thou hast spoken words reproachful,
Doubting of his soul's salvation,
Of his creed I never question'd,
But where'er he goes, I follow.
Whatsoe'er his lot, I'll share it,
Though it were the darkest chamber
In the lowest hell. 'Twere better
There with him, than 'mid the carols
Of the highest heaven, without him."

Swan-like arms were wrapped around her
With a cry of better pleading,
"Oh Miranda!—Oh my Sister!
Gather back the words you've spoken,
Quickly, ere the angel write them
Weeping on the doom's day tablet.

—You have grieved our blessed Mother:
See you not the large tears trickle
Down those channels deeply furrow'd
Which the widow-anguish open'd?
Kneel beside me, Oh my Sister!
Darling of my cradle slumbers,
Ask the grace of God to cleanse thee
From thy blasphemy and blindness,
Supplicate the Great Enlightener
Here to purge away thy madness,
Pray our Saviour to forgive thee."

"Bertha! Bertha! speak not to me,
What knowest thou of love almighty?
Naught except that craven spirit
Measuring, weighing, calculating,
That goes shivering to its bridal.
On this deathless soul, all hazard
Here I take, and if it perish,
Let it perish.
From the socket
This right eye I'd pluck, extinguish

This right hand, if he desire it,
And go maim'd through all the ages
That Eternity can number.

—Prayer is not for me, but action,
Against thee, and Her who bare me
Stand I at Love's bidding, boldly
In the armor that he giveth,
For life's battle, strong and ready.
—Hush! I've sworn, and I'll confirm it."

In due time, the handsome suitor
Paid his devoirs to Miranda,
In her own paternal dwelling.
Very exquisite in costume,
Very confident in manner,
Pompous, city-bred, and fearless
Was the accepted Aldebaran.

—Anxious felt she, lest the customs
Of the rustic race around her,
So she styled her rural neighbors,
Might discourage or disgust him,
But he gave them no attention,
Quite absorbed in other matters.

—In their promenades together
She beheld the people watching
Mid their toils of agriculture,

Saw them gaze from door and windows,
Little ones from gates and fences,
On the stylish Alderbaran,
And her heart leap'd up exulting.

—Notice took he of the homestead,
With an eye of speculation,
Ask'd the number of its acres,
And what revenue they yielded.
Notice took of herds and buildings
With their usufruct, and value,
Closer note than seem'd consistent
With his delicate position;
But Miranda, Cupid blinded,
No venality detected.

—He, in gorgeous phrase address'd her,
With an oriental worship,
As some goddess condescending
To an intercourse with mortals.
Pleas'd was she with such observance,
Pleas'd and proud that those around her
Should perceive what adoration
Was to her, by him accorded.

—When he left, 'twas with the assurance
The next visit should be final.
Marking on his silver tablet
With gay hand, the day appointed

When he might return to claim her
In the nuptial celebration.

There's a bridal in the spring-time,
When the bee from wintry covert
Talking to the unsheath'd blossoms,
Meditates unbounded plunder,
And the bird mid woven branches
Brooding o'er her future treasures
Harkeneth thrilling to the love-song
Of her mate, who nestward tendeth.

—There's a bridal in the spring-time,
And the beautiful Miranda
Through her veil of silvery tissue
Gleams, more beautiful than ever.
From the hearth-stone of her fathers,
With the deathless love of woman
Trusting all for earth or heaven
To a mortal's rule and guidance,
One, but short time since, a stranger,
Forth she goes.
The young beholders
Gazing on the handsome bridegroom,
Gazing on the nuptial carriage,
Where the milk-white horses sported
Knots of evergreen and myrtle,
Felt a pleasure mix'd with envy
At a happiness so perfect.

—But more thoughtful ones, instructed
By the change of time and sorrow,
By the cloud and by the sunbeam,
Felt the hazard that attended
Such intrustment without limit,
Vows that none had right to cancel
Save the hand of Death's dark Angel.

Of the sadness left behind her
In the mansion whence she parted,
Loneliness, and bitter heart-ache,
Deep, unutter'd apprehension,
Fearful looking for of judgment,
It were vain in lays so feeble
To attempt a true recital.

—Still, to Mother and to Sister
Came epistles from Miranda,
Essenc'd and genteelly written,
Painting happiness so perfect,
So transcending expectation,
So surpassing all that fancy
In her wildest flights had pencil'd,
That even Eden ere the tempter
Coil'd himself amid the blossoms
Fail'd to furnish fitting symbol.

Heartfelt bliss is never boastful,
Like the holy dew it stealeth

To the bosom of the violet,
Only told by deeper fragrance.

—He who saith "See! see! I'm happy?
Happier than all else around me,"
Leaves, perchance, a doubt behind him
Whether he hath comprehended
What true happiness implieth.

Oh, the storm-cloud and the tempest!
Oh, the dreary night of winter!
Drifting snows, and winds careering
Down the tall, wide-throated chimney,
Like the shrieking ghosts from Hades.
Shrieking ghosts of buried legions.

—"Mother! hear I not the wailing
Of a human voice?"
"My daughter!
'Tis the blast that rends the pine-trees.
The old sentry-Oak is broken,
Close beside our chamber-window,
And its branches all are moaning.
'Tis their grief you hear, my daughter."

But the maiden's ear was quicken'd
To all plaint of mortal sorrow,
And when next, the bitter north wind

Lull'd, to gather strength and vigor,
For a new exacerbation,
Listening close, she caught the murmur,
"Hush mein daughter! hush mein baby."
Then she threw the door wide open,
Though the storm rush'd in upon her,
With its blinding sleet and fury.

What beheld she, near the threshold,
Prostrate there beside the threshold,
But a woman, to whose bosom
Clung a young and sobbing infant?

—Oh the searching look that kindled
'Neath those drooping, straining eye-lids,
Searching mid the blast and darkness,
For some helper in her anguish,
Searching, kindling look, that settled
Into heavy, deadly slumber,
As the waning taper flashes
Once, to be relumin'd never.

Still her weak arm clasp'd the baby,
Rais'd its pining, pinching features,
Faintly cried, "Mein kind! Have pity,
Pity, for the love of Jesus!"

—Yes, forlorn, benighted wanderer,
Thy poor, failing feet have brought thee
Where the love of Jesus dwelleth.

Gently in a bed they laid her,
Chafed her stiffening limbs and temples,
Pour'd the warm, life-giving cordial,
But what seem'd the most to cheer her,
Were some words by Bertha spoken
In her own, dear native language.
Voice of Fatherland! it quicken'd
All the heart's collapsing heart-strings,
As though bath'd, and renovated
In the Rhine's blue, rushing waters.

O'er the wildering waste of ocean,
Moved by zeal of emigration
She had ventured with her husband
To this western World of promise,
Rainbow-vested El-Dorado.

On that dreary waste of waters
He had died, and left her mourning,
All unguided, unbefriended.
—There the mother-sorrow found her
And compell'd her by the weeping
Of the new-born, to encounter
With a broken-hearted welcome
Life once more, which in the torrent
Of her utter desolation
She had cast aside, contemning
As a burden past endurance.

—Outcast in this land of strangers,
Strange of speech, and strange in manner,
She had travel'd, worn and weary,
Here and there, with none to aid her,
Ask'd for work, and none employ'd her,
Ask'd for alms, and few reliev'd her,
Till at length, the wintry tempest
Smote her near that blessed roof-tree.

Heavy slumber weigh'd her downward,
Slumber from whence none awaketh.
Yet at morn they heard her sighing,
On her pillow faintly sighing,
"I am ready! I am ready!"
"Leonore! my child! my darling!"

Then they brought the infant to her,
Cleanly robed, and sweetly smiling,
And the parting soul turn'd backward,
And the clay-seal on the eyelids
Lifted up to gaze upon it.

Bertha kiss'd the little forehead,
Said "*mein kind*," and lo! a shudder
Of this earth's forgotten pleasure
Trembled o'er the dying woman,
And the white hand cold as marble
Strove to raise itself in blessing,
For the mother-joy was stronger

That one moment, while it wrestled
With the pausing king of terrors,
Stronger than the king of terrors.

Then they laid her icy fingers
Mid the infant's budding ringlets,
And the pang and grasp subsided
In a smile and whispering cadence,
"God, mein God, be praised!"—and silence
Settled on those lips forever.

Favor'd is the habitation
Where a gentle infant dwelleth,
When its brightening eye revealeth
The immortal part within it,
And its curious wonder scanneth
All its wide spread, tiny fingers,
And its velvet hand caressing
Pats the nurse's cheek and bosom,
Hoary Age grows young before it,
As the branch that Winter blighted
At the touch of Spring reviveth.

When its healthful form evolveth,
And with quadrupedal pleasure
Creeping o'er the nursery carpet,
Aiming still, its flowery surface
With faint snatches to appropriate,
Or the bolder art essaying
On its two round feet to balance

And propel the swaying body
As with outstretch'd arms it hastens
Tottering toward the best beloved,
Hope, her freshest garland weaveth
Glittering with the dews of morning.

When the lisping tongue adventures
The first tones of imitation,
Or with magic speed o'ermasters
The philosophy of language
Twining round the mind of others,
Preferences, and pains and pleasures,
Tendrils strong, of sentient being,
Seeking kindness and indulgence,
Loving sports and smiles, and gladness,
Tenderest love goes forth to meet it,
Love that every care repayeth.

Thus the little German exile
Leaning on her foster parents
Brought a love that soothed and cheer'd them,
And with sweet confiding meekness
Taught to older ones the lesson
Of the perfect trust, we children
Of One Great Almighty Parent
Should repose in His protection
Goodness and unerring wisdom:
Though His discipline mysterious
Oft transcendeth feeble reason,

And perchance overthrows the fabrics
That in arrogance we builded,
Call'd *our own*, and vainly rented
To a troop of hopes and fancies,
Gay-robed joys, or fond affections.

'Tis a solemn thing and lovely,
To adopt a child, whose mother
Dwelleth in the land of spirits:
In its weakness give it succor,
Be in ignorance its teacher,
In all sorrow its consoler,
In temptation its defender,
Save what else had been forsaken,
Win for it a crown in Heaven,—
Tis a solemn thing and lovely,
Such a work as God approveth.

Blessed are the souls that nurture
With paternal care the orphan,
Neath their roof-tree lending shelter,
At their table breathing welcome,
Giving armor for the journey
And the warfare that awaiteth
Every pilgrim, born of woman,
Blessed, for the grateful prayer
Riseth unto Him who heareth
The lone sigh of the forsaken,

Bendeth, mid the song of seraphs,
To the crying of the ravens,
From whose nest the brooding pinion
By the archer's shaft was sever'd.

Pomp and wealth, and pride of office
With their glitter and their shouting,
May not pass through death's dark valley,
May not thrill the ear that resteth
Mid the silence of the grave-yard;
But the deed that wrought in pity
Mid the outcast and benighted,
In the hovel or the prison,
On the land or on the ocean,
Shunning still the applause of mortals,
Comes it not to His remembrance
Who shall say amid the terrors
Of the last Great Day of Judgment,
" Inasmuch as ye have done it
Unto one, the least, the lowest,
It was done to Me, your Saviour."

CANTO THIRD.

I'LL change my measure, and so end my lay,
Too long already.
I can't manage well
The metre of that master of the lyre,
Who Hiawatha, and our forest tribes
Deftly described. Hexameters, I hate,
And henceforth do eschew their company,
For what is written irksomely, will be
Read in like manner.
What did I say last
In my late canto? Something, I believe
Of gratitude.
Now this same gratitude
Is a fine word to play on. Many a niche
It fills in letters, and in billet-doux,—
Its adjective a graceful prefix makes
To a well-written signature. It gleams
A happy mirage in a sunny brain;
But as a principle, is oft, I fear,
Inoperative. Some satirist hath said
That *gratitude is only a keen sense*
Of future favors.

10*

As regards myself,
Tis my misfortune, and perhaps, my fault,
Yet I'm constrain'd to say, that where my gifts
And efforts have been greatest, the return
Has been in contrast. So that I have shrunk
To grant myself the pleasure of great love
Lest its reward might be indifference,
Or smooth deceit. Others no doubt have been
More fortunate. I trust 'tis often so:
But this is my experience, on the scale
Of three times twenty years, and somewhat more.

In that calm happiness which Virtue gives,
Blent with the daily zeal of doing good,
Mother and daughter dwelt.
Once, as they came
From their kind visit to a child of need,
Cheered by her blessings,—at their home they found
Miranda and her son. With rapid speech,
And strong emotion that resisted tears
Her tale she told. Forsaken were they both,
By faithless sire and husband. He had gone
To parts unknown, with an abandon'd one
He long had follow'd. Brokenly she spake
Of taunts and wrongs long suffer'd and conceal'd
With woman's pride. Then bitterly she pour'd
Her curses on his head.
With shuddering tears
They press'd her to their hearts.

"Come back! Come back!
To your first home, and Heaven's compassions heal
Your wounded spirit."
Lovingly they cast
Their mantle o'er her, striving to uplift
Her thoughts to heavenly sources, and allure
To deeds of charity, that draw the sting
From selfishness of sorrow."
But she shrank
From social intercourse, nor took her seat
Even in the House of God, lest prying eyes
Should gloat upon her downfall. Books, nor work
Enticed her, and the lov'd piano's tone
Waking sad echoes of the days that were,
She seem'd to shun. Her joy was in her child.
The chief delight and solace of her life
To adorn his dress, and trim his shining curls,
Dote on his beauty, and conceal his faults,
With weak indulgence.
"Oh, Miranda, love!
Teach your fair boy, obedience. 'Tis the first
Lesson of life. To him, you fill the place
Of that Great Teacher who doth will us all
To learn submission."
But Miranda will'd
In her own private mind, not to adopt
Such old-world theories, deeming the creed
Of the grey-headed Mother, obsolete.
—Her boy was fair; but in those manners fail'd

That render beauty pleasing. Great regard
Had he for self, and play, and dainty food,
Unlike those Jewish children, who refused
The fare luxurious of Chaldea's king,
And on their simple diet grow more fair
And healthful than their mates, and wiser too,
Than the wise men of Babylon.
I've seen
Ill-fortune follow those, whose early tastes
Were pampered and inured to luxury.
Their palates seem'd to overtop the brain,
And the rank Dives-pleasure, to subvert
Childhood's simplicity of sweet content.
—Precocious appetites, when overruled,
Or disappointed, lend imperious strength
To evil tempers, and a fierce disdain.
Methought, our Mother-Land, in this respect
Had wiser usages. Her little ones
At their own regular, plain table learn'd
No culinary criticism, nor claim'd
Admission to the richly furnish'd board
Nor deem'd the viands of their older friends
Pertain'd to them.

A pleasant sight it was
At close of day, their simple supper o'er,
To find them in the quiet nursery laid,
Like rose-buds folded in a fragrant sheath
To peaceful slumber. Hence their nerves attain'd
Firm texture, and the key-stone of the frame,

This wondrous frame, so often sinn'd against,—
Unwarp'd and undispeptic, gave to life
A higher zest.
Year after year swept by,
And Conrad's symmetry of form and face
Grew more conspicuous. Yet he fail'd to win
Approval from the pious, or desire
To seek him as companion for their sons.

—At school and college he defied restraint,
And round the associates of his idle hours
Threw a mysterious veil. But rumor spake
Of them, as those who would be sure to bring
Disgrace and infamy.
Strong thirst for gold
Sprang with the weeds of vice. His mother's purse
Was drain'd for him, and when at length she spake
In warm remonstrance, he with rudeness rush'd
Out of her presence, or withdrew himself
All night from her abode. Then she was fain
To appease his anger by some lavish gift
From scant resources, which she ill could spare,
Making the evil worse.
The growth of sin
Is rank and rapid when the youthful heart
Abjures the sway of duty. Weaving oft
The mesh of falsehood, may it not forget
What the truth is? The wavering, moral sense
Depraved and weaken'd, fails to grasp the clue

Of certainty, nor scruples to deny
Words utter'd, and deeds done, for conscience sleeps
Stifled, and callous. Fearful must it be,
When Truth offended and austere, confronts
The false soul at Heaven's bar.

An aged man
Dwelt by himself upon a dreary moor,
And it was whisper'd that a miser's hoard
Absorb'd his thoughts.

There, at the midnight hour
The unwonted flash of lights was seen by those
Who chanced to pass, and entering in, they found
The helpless inmate murder'd in his bed,
And the house rifled.

Differing tracks they mark'd
Of flying footsteps in the moisten'd soil,
And eager search ensued.

At length, close hid
In a dense thicket, Conrad they espied,
His shoes besmear'd with blood. Question'd of those
Who with him in this work of horror join'd,
He answered nothing.

All unmov'd he stood
Upon his trial, the nefarious deed
Denying, and of his accomplices
Disclosing nought. But still there seem'd a chain
Of evidence to bind him in its coil,
And Justice had her course. The prison bolts

Closed heavily behind him, and his doom
For years, with felons was incorporate.

Of the wild anguish and despair that reign'd
In his ancestral home, no words can give
Description meet.
In the poor mother's mind
Reason forsook its throne. Her last hope gone,
Torn by a torrent from her death-like grasp,
Having no anchor on the eternal Rock,
She plunged beside it, into gulphs profound.
—She slept not, ate not, heeded no kind word,
Caress of fondness, or benignant prayer:
She only shriek'd,
"My boy! my beautiful!
They bind his hands!"
And then with frantic cries
She struggled 'gainst imaginary foes,
Till strength was gone.
Through the long syncope
Her never-resting lips essay'd to form
The gasping sounds,
"My boy! my beautiful!
Hence! Caitiffs! hence! my boy! my beautiful!"
And in that unquell'd madness life went out,
Like lamp before the blast.

With sullen port
Of bravery, as one who scorns defeat

Though it hath come upon him, Conrad met
The sentence of the law. But its full force
He fail'd to estimate; the stern restraint
On liberty of movement, coarsest fare,
Stripes for the contumacious, and for all
Labor, and silence.
The inquiring glance
On the new-comer bent, from stolid eyes
Of malefactors, harden'd to their lot,
And hating all mankind, he coldly shunn'd
Or haughtily return'd. Yet there were lights
Even in this dark abode, not often found
In penal regions, where the wrath of man
Is prompt to punish, and remembereth not
The mercy that himself doth ask of God.

—A just man was the warden and humane,
Not credulous, or easily deceiv'd,
But hopeful of our nature, though deprav'd,
And for the incarcerate, careful to restrain
All petty tyranny.
Courteous was he
To visitants, for many such there were.
Philanthropists, whose happy faith believ'd
Prisons reforming schools, came here to scan
Arrangements and appliances as guides
To other institutions: strangers too,
Who 'mid their explorations of the State,
Scenery and structures, would not overlook
Its model-prison.

Now and then, was seen
Some care-worn mother, leading by the hand
Her froward boy, with hope that he might learn
A lesson from the punishment he saw.

—When day was closed and to his narrow cell
Bearing his supper, every prisoner went,
The night-lock firmly clench'd, beside some grate
While the large lamp thro' the long corridors
Threw flickering light, the Chaplain often stood
Conversing. Of the criminal's past life
He made inquiry, and receiv'd replies
Foreign from truth, or vague and taciturn:
And added pious counsels, unobserv'd,
Heeded but slightly, or ill understood.

The leaden-footed weeks o'er Conrad pass'd,
With deadening weight.
Privation bow'd his pride.
The lily-handed, smiting at the forge,
Detested life, and meditated means
To accomplish suicide.
At dusk of eve,
While in his cell, on darkest themes he mused,
Before his grate, a veiled woman stood.

—She spake not, but her presence made him glad,—
A purer atmosphere seem'd breathing round
To expand his shrivell'd heart.

Fair gifts she brought,
Roses fresh-blown, and cates, and fragrant fruits
Most grateful to his fever'd lip.
"Oh speak!
Speak to me!"
But she glided light away,
And heavenly sweet, her parting whisper said
"Good night! With the new moon I'll come again."

"With the new Moon!"
Hope! hope! Its magic wand
With phosphorescence ting'd that Stygian pool
Of chill despair, in which his soul had sank
Lower and lower still. Now, at the forge
A blessed vision gleam'd. Its mystery woke
The romance of his nature. Every day
Moved lighter on, and when he laid it down,
It breathed "*good night!*" like a complacent child
Going to rest. One barrier less remain'd
Between him and the goal, and to each night
A tarrying, tedious guest, he bade farewell,
Like lover, counting toward his spousal-morn.

But *will she come?*
And then, he blamed the doubt.
His pulse beat quicker, as the old moon died.
And when the slender sickle of pale gold
Cut the blue concave, by his grated door

Stood the veil'd visitant. The breath of flowers
Foretold her coming. With their wealth she brought
Grapes in the cluster, and a clasped Book,
The holiest, and the best.
"Show me thine eyes!"
He pray'd. But still with undrawn veil, she gave
The promise of return, in whisper sweet,
"Good night! good night!
Wilt read my Book? and say
Oh Lamb of God, forgive!"
So, by the lamp
When tardy Evening still'd the din of toil,
He read of Him who came to save the lost,
Who touch'd the blind, and they receiv'd their sight,
The dead young man, and raised him from his bier,
Reproved the raging Sea, and it was still:
Deeds that his boyhood heard unheedingly.
But here, in this strange solitude of pain
With different voice they spake. And as he read,
The fragrance of the mignionette he loved,
Press'd 'tween the pages, lured him onward still.

Now, a new echo in his heart was born,
And sometimes mid the weary task, and leer
Of felon faces, ere he was aware
From a compress'd unmurmuring lip, it broke,
O Lamb of God! If still unquell'd Despair
Thrust up a rebel standard, down it fell
At the o'er-powering sigh, *O Lamb of God!*

And ere upon his pallet low, he sank,
It sometimes breathed, " *O Lamb of God, forgive!*
Like the taught lesson of a humbled child.

Yet duly as the silver vested moon
Hiding awhile in the dark breast of night
Return'd to take her regent watch again
Over our sleeping planet, softly came
That shrouded visitant, preferring still
Like those who guard us lest we dash our foot
Against a stone, to do her blessed work
Unseen. And with the liberal gifts she brought
For body, and for soul, there seem'd to float
A legacy of holy themes and thoughts
Behind her, like an incense-stream. He mused
Oft-times of patience, and the dying love
Of our dear Lord, nor yet without remorse
Of that unsullied Truth which Vice rejects,
And God requires.
How beautiful is Truth!
Her right-lined course, amid the veering curves
And tangents of the world, her open face
Seeking communion with the scanning stars,
Her grave, severe simplicity of speech
Untrammelled by the wiles of rhetoric,
By bribes of popular applause unbow'd,
In unison with Him she dwells who ruled
The tyranny of Chaos, with the words

"*Let there be light!*"

Gladly we turn again
To that fair mansion mid the rural vales
Where first our song awoke. Advancing years
Brought to its blessed Lady no regret
Or weak complaint for what the hand of Time
Had borne away. Enduring charms were hers
On which he laid no tax; the beaming smile,
The voice of melody, the hand that mark'd
Each day with deeds of goodness, and the heart
That made God's gift of life more beautiful,
The more prolong'd. Its griefs she counted gains,
Since He who wisely will'd them cannot err,
And loves while He afflicts.

Their dialect
Was breathed in secret 'tween her soul and Him.
But toward mankind, her duties made more pure
By the strong heat of their refining fires,
Flow'd forth like molten gold. She sought the poor,
Counsell'd the ignorant, consoled the sad,
And made the happy happier, by her warmth
Of social sympathy. She loved to draw
The young around her table; well she knew
To cheer and teach them, by the tale or song,
Or sacred hymn, for music dwelt with her
Till life went out. It pleased her much to hear
Their innocent merriment, while from the flow
And swelling happiness of childhood's heart
So simply purchased, she herself imbibed

A fuller tide of fresh vitality.
Her favor'd guests exultingly rehears'd
Their visits to "the Lady," counting each
A privilege, not having learned the creed
Which modern times inculcate in our land
That whatsoe'er is *old*, is *obsolete*.

—Still ever at her side, by night and day
Was Bertha, entering into every plan,
With zealous aid, assuming every care
That brought a burden, catching every smile
On the clear mirror of a loving heart,
Which by reflection doubled. Thus they dwelt,
Mother and daughter, in sweet fellowship,
One soul betwixt them. Filial piety
Thrives best with generous natures. Here was nought
Of self to check it, so it richly bloom'd
Like the life-tree, that yieldeth every month
New fruits, still hiding mid its wealth of leaves
The balm of healing.
In that peaceful home
The fair-haired orphan was a fount of joy,
Spreading her young heart like a tintless sheet
For Love to write on. Sporting 'mid the flowers,
Caroling with the birds, or gliding light
As fawn, her fine, elastic temperament
Took happiest coloring from each varying hour
Or changing duty. Kind, providing cares
Which younglings often thoughtlessly receive

Or thankless claim, she gratefully repaid
With glad obedience. Pleas'd was she to bear
Precocious part in household industry,
Round shining bars to involve the shortening thread,
And see the stocking grow, or side by side
With her loved benefactresses to work
Upon some garment for the ill-clad poor,
With busy needle. As their almoner,
'Twas her delight to seek some lowly hut
And gliding thence, with noiseless footstep, leave
With her kind dole, a wonder whence it came.
—A heavenly blessing wrapp'd its wing around
The adopted orphanage.

Oh ye whose homes
Are childless, know ye not some little heart
Collapsing, for the need of parent's love,
That ye might breathe upon? some outcast lamb
That ye might shelter in your fold? content
To make the sad eye sparkle, guide the feet
In duty's path, bring a new soul to Heaven,
And take your payment from the Judge's Voice,
At the Last Day?

—A tireless tide of joy,
A world of pleasure in the garden bound,
Open'd to Leonore. From the first glance
Of the frail Crocus through its snowy sheath,
On, to the ripen'd gatherings of the Grape,
And thorn-clad chestnut, all was sweet to her.
She loved to plant the seed and watch the germ,

And nurse the tender leaflet like a babe,
And lead the tendril right. To her they seem'd
Like living friends. She sedulously mark'd
Their health and order, and was skill'd to prune
The too luxuriant spray, or gadding vine.
She taught the blushing Strawberry where to run,
And stoop'd to kiss the timid Violet,
Blossoming in the shade, and sometimes dream'd
The Lily of the lakelet, calmly throned
On its broad leaf, like Moses in his ark,
Spake words to her. And so, as years fled by,
Young Fancy, train'd by Nature, turn'd to God.
Her clear, Teutonic mind, took hold on truth
And found in every season, change of joy.

—Yet her prime pleasure seem'd at wintry eve
Tho' storms might fall, when from its branching arms
The antique candelabra shed fair light
On polished wainscot and rich curtains dropp'd
Close o'er the casements, she might draw her seat
Near to her aged friend and take her hand
And frame her voice to join some tuneful song,
Treasuring whate'er of wise remark distill'd
From those loved lips.
Then, as her Mentor spoke
Of God's great goodness in this mortal life,
Teaching us both by sorrow and by joy,
And how we ought to yield it back with trust
And not with dread, whenever He should call,
Having such precious promises, through Christ

Of gain unspeakable, beyond the grave,
The listening pupil felt her heart expand
With reverent love.
Friendship, 'tween youth and age
Is gain to both,—nor least to that which finds
The germs of knowledge and experience drop
And twine themselves around the unfrosted locks,
A fadeless coronet. In this sweet home
The lengthen'd day seem'd short for their delights,
And wintry evening brief. The historic page
Made vocal, brought large wealth to memory.
The lore of distant climes, that rose and fell
Ere our New World, like Lazarus came forth,
The napkin round her forehead, and sate down
Beside her startled sisters.
Last of all,
The large time-honor'd Bible loos'd its clasps
And shed its manna on their waiting souls;
Then rose the sacred hymn in blended tones,
By Bertha's parlor-organ made intense
In melody of praise, and fervent Prayer
Set its pure crown upon the parted day,
And kiss'd the Angel, Sleep.
Yet ere they rose
From bended knee, there was a lingering pause,
A silent orison for one whose name
But seldom pass'd their lips, though in their hearts
His image with its faults and sorrows dwelt,
Invoking pity of a pardoning God.

—Thus fled the years away, the cultured glebe
Stirr'd by the vernal plough-share, yielding charms
To Summer, pouring wealth o'er Autumn's breast,
Pausing from weary toil, when Winter comes,
Bringing its Sabbath, as the man of eld
With snow upon his temples, peaceful sits
In his arm-chair, to ruminate and rest.

Once, at that season when the ices shrink
Befere the vernal equinox, at morn
There was no movement in the Lady's room,
Who prized the early hours like molten gold,
And ever rose before the kingly Sun.

—On the white pillow still reposed her head,
Her cheek upon her hand. She had retired
In health, affection's words, and trustful prayers
Hallowing her lips. Now, on her brow there seem'd
Unwonted smoothness, and the smile was there
Set as a seal, with which the call she heard,
"*Come! sister-spirit!*"
She had gain'd the wish
Oft utter'd to her God, to pass away
Without the sickness and enfeebled powers
That tax the heart of love. Death that unbars
Unto the ready soul the Gate of Heaven,
Claiming no pang or groan from failing flesh,
Doth angel-service.
But alas! the shock,
The chill, the change, the anguish, where she dwelt,

And must return no more. As one amaz'd
The stricken daughter held her breath for awe,
God seem'd so near. Methought she saw the Hand
That smote her. Half herself was reft away,
Body and soul. Yet no repining word
Announc'd her agony.
                                        The tolling bell
To hill and valley, told with solemn tongue
That death had been among them, and at door
And window listening, aged crone and child
Counted its strokes, a stroke for every year,
And predicated thence, as best they might,
Whom they had lost. Neighbor of neighbor ask'd,
Till the sad tidings were possess'd by all.

—A village funeral is a thing that warns
All from their homes. In the throng'd city's bound,
Hearses unnoticed pass, and none inquire
Who goeth to his grave. But rural life
Keepeth afresh the rills of sympathy.
True sorrow was there at these obsequies,
For all the poor were mourners. There the old
Came in the garments she had given, bow'd down
With their own sense of loss. O'er furrow'd cheeks
In care-worn channels stole the trickling tear.
The young were weepers, for their memories stored
Many a gentle word, and precept kind,
Like jewels dropp'd behind her. Mothers rais'd
Their little ones above the coffin's side

To look upon her face. Lingering they gazed
Deeming the lovely Lady sweetly slept
Among the flowers that on her pillow lay.

He's but a tyro in the school of grief
Who hath not from the victor-tomb return'd
Unto his rifled home. The utter weight
Of whelming desolation doth not fall
Till the last rites are paid. The cares of love
Having no longer scope, withdraw their shield,
And even the seat whereon the lost one sate,
The pen he held, the cup from which he drank,
Launch their keen darts against the festering soul.

—The lonely daughter, never since her birth
Divided from the mother, having known
No separate pleasure, or secreted thought,
With deep humility resumed her course
Of daily duty and philanthropy,
Not murmuring, but remembering His great love
Who lent so long that blessing beyond price,
And from her broken censer offering still
Incense of praise.
She deem'd it fearful loss
To lose a sorrow, be chastis'd in vain,
Not yield our joys, but have them rent away,
And make this life a battle-field with God.

The sombre shadow brooding o'er their home
Was felt by all. The heart of Leonore

Dwindled and shrank beneath it. Vigor fled,
The untasted meal, and couch bedew'd with tears
Gave the solution to her wasted flesh,
And drooping eye-lids.
Folded in her arms,
Bertha with tender accents said, "my child,
We please not her who to the angels went,
By hopeless grief. Doubt not her watchful eye
Regards us, though unseen. How oft she taught
To make God's will our own. You, who were glad
To do her bidding then, distress her not
By disobedience now. Waste not the health
In reckless martyrdom, which Heaven hath link'd
With many duties, and with hope to dwell
If faithful found, with Her who went before
And beckoning waits us."
From dull trance of grief
By kind reproof awakened, Leonore
Strove to redeem her scholarship from blame
And be a comforter, as best she might
To her remaining patroness.

Within
The limits of a neighboring town, a wretch
Fell by the wayside, struck by sudden Death
That vice propels. A Man of God, who sought
Like his blest Master every form of woe
Found him, and to a shelter and a couch
Convey'd. Then bending down, with earnest words

For time grew short, he urg'd him to repent.
"Say, Lord have mercy on my soul.
Look up
Unto the Lamb of God, for He can save
Even to the uttermost."
Slight heed obtain'd
This adjuration, wild the glazing eye
Fix'd on the wall,—and ever and anon
The stiffening fingers clutch'd at things unseen,
While from those spent lungs came a shuddering sound,
"*That's he! That's he!*
The old man! His grey hairs
Dabbled with blood!"
Then in a loud, long cry,
Wrung out by torturing pain,
"I struck the blow!
I tell ye that I struck the blow, and scaped.
Conrad who bore the doom is innocent,
Save fellowship with guilt."
And so he fled;
The voice of prayer around him, but the soul
Beyond its reach. The kneeling Pastor rose
Sadly, as when the Shepherd fails to snatch
A wanderer from the Lion.
But the truth
Couch'd in that dismal cry of parting life
He treasured up, and bore to those who held
Power to investigate and to reprieve;
And authorized by them with gladness sought

The gloomy prison. Conrad there he found
In sullen syncope of sickening thought,
And cautiously in measured terms disclosed
His liberation. Wondering doubt look'd forth
From eyes that opening wide and wider still
Strain'd from their sockets. Yet the hand he took
That led him from the cell, and onward moved
Like Peter following his angel guide
Deeming he saw a vision. As the bolts
Drew gratingly to let them pass, he seem'd
To gather consciousness, and restless grew
With an unspoken fear, lest at the last
Some sterner turnkey, or gruff sentinel
Might bar their egress.
When behind them closed.
The utmost barrier, and the sweet, fresh air
So long witheld, fill'd his collapsing lungs,
He shouted rapturously,
"*Am I alive?*
Or have I burst the gates of death, and found
A second Eden?"
The unwonted sound
Of his own voice, freed from the drear constraint
Of prison durance, swell'd his thrilling frame
With strong and joyous impulse, for 'tis said
Long stifled utterance is torturing pain
To organs train'd to speech.
With one high leap
Like an enfranchis'd steed he seem'd to throw
His spirit-chain behind him. Then he took

The Pastor's offer'd arm, who led the way
To his own house, and bade him bathe and change
His prison garments, and repose that night
Under his roof.
                                        With thoughtful care he spoke
To his own household, kindly to receive
The erring one,—"for we are sinners all,
And not upon our merits may depend
But on abounding grace."
                                        So when the hour
Of cheerful supper summon'd to the board,
He came among them as a comely guest,
Refresh'd and welcome. Pleasant converse cheer'd
The hospitable meal, and then withdrawn
Into the quiet study 'mid the books,
That saintly good man with the hoary hair
Silvering his temples like a graceful crown,
Strove by wise counsel to encourage him
For life's important duties,
                                        But he deem'd
A ban was on him, and a mark which all
Would scan who met him.
                                        "He whose lot hath been
With fiends in Pandemonium, must expect
Hate and contempt from men."
                                        "Not so, my son!
Wipe off the past, as a forgotten thing,
Propitiate virtue, by forsaking vice.
The good will aid you, and a brighter day

Doubtless awaits you. Be not too much moved
By man's applause or blamé, but ever look
Unto a higher Judge."
                    Then there arose
A voice of supplication, so intense
To the Great Pardoner, that He would send
His spirit down to change and purify
The erring heart, that those persuasive tones,
So humble, yet so strangely eloquent
Breathed o'er the unhappy one like soothing spell
Of magic influence, and he slept that night
With peace and hope, long exiled from his couch.

A summer drive to one sequestered long,
Hath charms untold.
                    The common face of earth,
The waving grass, the rustle of the leaves,
Kiss'd by the zephyr, or by winged bird
Disparted, as it finds its chirping nest,
The murmur of the brooks, the low of herds,
The ever-changing landscape, rock and stream,
And azure concave fleck'd with silver clouds
Awaken rapturous joy. This Conrad felt,
While pleasure every kindling feature touch'd,
And every accent tuned. But when they saw
The fair ancestral roof through trees afar,
Strong agony convuls'd him, and he cried,
"*Not there! Not there!*

First take me to *Her* grave!"
And so to that secluded spot they turn'd,
Where rest the silent dead.
On the green mound,
His Mother's bed, with sobs and groans he fell,
And in his paroxysm of grief would fain
Have torn the turf-bound earth away, to reach
The mouldering coffin. Then, a flood of tears,
Heaven's blessed gift burst forth,
"Oh weep, my Son!
These gushing tears shall help to wash away
Remorseful pangs, and lurking seeds of sin.
Here, in this sacred tomb, bury the past,
And strong in heavenly trust, resolve to rise
To a new life."
Still kneeling on the sod
With hands and eyes uprais'd, he said,
"*I will!*
So help me God!"
The tear was on his cheek
Undry'd, when to the home of peace they came.
There Bertha greeted them with outstretch'd hands
And beaming brow, while the good Pastor said,
"Thy Son was dead, but is alive again."
A sweet voice answer'd,
"Lost he was, and found!
Oh, welcome home."
She would have folded him
In her embrace. But at her feet he fell,

Clasping her knees, and bowing down his head,
Till she assured him that a mother's love
Was in her heart.
"And there is joy in Heaven
Because of him, this day," the good Man said.
—His tones were tremulous, as up he rose,
"Ah, my veil'd Angel! Now I see thy face,
And hear thy voice."

What were the glowing thoughts
Of the meek shepherd, as alone he took
His homeward way? The joy of others flow'd
O'er his glad spirit like a refluent tide
Whose sands were gold. Had he not chosen well
His source of happiness?
There are, who mix
Pride and ambition with their services
Before the altar. Did the tinkling bells
Upon the garments of the Jewish priest
Draw down his thoughts from God?
The mitred brow,
Doth it stoop low enough to find the souls
That struggle in the pits of sin, and die?
Methinks ambitious honors might disturb
The man whose banner is the Cross of Christ,
And earth's high places shut him out of Heaven.

—Yet this serene disciple, so content
To do his Master's will, in humblest works

Of charity, had he not chosen well
His happiness?
The hero hears the trump
Of victor-fame, and his high pulses leap,
But laurels dipp'd in blood shall vex his soul
When the death-ague comes. More blest is he
Who bearing on his brow the anointing oil
Keeps in his heart the humility and zeal
That sanctify his vows. So, full of joy
That fears no frost of earth, because its root
Is by the river of eternal life,
The white-hair'd Pastor took his homeward way.

New life upon the farm. A master's eye
And step are there. Forest, and cultured field,
And garden feel his influence. Forth at morn
He goes amid the laboring hinds who bathe
Their scythe in fragrant dew, mid all their toils
Teaching or learning, with such cheerful port
As won their hearts.
Even animals partook
His kind regard. The horse, with arching neck,
And ear erect, replied as best he might
To his caressing tones. The patient ox,
With branching horns, and the full-udder'd cow
Grew sleek and flourish'd and in happiest guise
Reveal'd his regency. The noble dog,
O'erflowing with intelligence and zeal,
Follow'd him as a friend; even the poor cat

Oft scorn'd and distanc'd, till her fawning love
Turns into abjectness, crept to his knee
Without reproof, and thro' her half-shut eyes
Regarding him, ere into sleep she sank
With song monotonous, express'd her joy.

—He loved to hear the clarion of the cock,
And see him in his gallantry protect
The brooding mothers,—of their infant charge
So fond and proud.
The generous care bestow'd
For weal and comfort of these servitors
And their mute dialect of gratitude
Pleas'd and refresh'd him, while those blessed toils
That quicken earth's fertility bestowed
The boon of healthful vigor. Bertha found
The burden of her cares securely laid
On his young arm, and gratefully beheld
Each day a portion of allotted time
Spent in the library, with earnest care,
Seeking the knowledge that in youth he scorn'd.

—Amid their rural neighborhood were some
Who frankly took him by the hand, as one,
Worthy to rise, and others who preferr'd
To cherish evil memories, or indulge
Dark auguries. But on his course he held
Unmov'd by either, for to her he seem'd
Intent and emulous alone to please
A higher Judge. When leaning on his arm

She sought the House of God, her tranquil brow
Seem'd in its time-tried beauty to express
The *Nunc Dimittis.*

Prisons are not oft
Converting places. Vicious habits shorn
Of their top branches, strike a rankling root
Darkly beneath, while hatred of mankind
And of the justice that decreed such doom
Bar out the Love Divine.

Yet Bertha felt
God's spirit was not limited, and might
Pluck brands from out the burning, and in faith
Believ'd the son of many prayers had found
Remission of his God. His life she scann'd,
Of honest, cheerful industry, combined
With intellectual progress, and perceived
How his religious worship humbly wore
The signet "*I have sinn'd;*" while toward men
His speech was cautious, far beyond his years,
As one by stern Experience school'd to know
The human heart's deceptions. Yet at home
And in that fellowship with Nature's works
Which Agriculture gives, his soul threw off
Its fetters and grew strong.

Once as they walk'd
Within a favorite grove, consulting where
The woodman's ax, or pruning-knife had best
Exert their wholesome ministry, he led
To a fair resting-place, a turf-bound seat,

Beneath a spreading Walnut, carpeted
With depth of fragrant leaves, while a slight brook
Half-hidden, half revealed, with minstrel touch,
Soften'd the spirit. There, in tones subdued
By strong emotion, he disclosed his love
For Leonore.
"Oh Conrad! she is pure
And peaceful as the lily bud that sleeps
On the heaven-mirror'd lake."
"I know it well,
Nor would I wake a ripple or a breath
To mar its purity."
"Yet wait, my Son!"
"*Wait? Mother, wait! It is not in man's heart
To love, and wait?*"
"But make your prayer to God.
Lay your petition at his feet, and see
What is His will."
"Before that God I swear
To be her true protector and best friend
Till death remove me hence, if she confide
At fitting time, that holy trust to me.
Oh angel Mother! sanction me to search
If in her heart there be one answering chord
To my great love. So may we lead below
That blended life which with a firmer step
And holier joy tends upward toward a realm
Of perfect bliss."

Thus authorized, he made
Her mind's improvement his delight, and found
Community in knowledge was a spell
To draw young hearts together. O'er the lore
And language of her native land they hung
Gleaning its riches with a tireless hand,
Deep and enamour'd students. When she sang
Or play'd, he join'd her with his silvery flute,
Making the thrill of music more intense
Through the heart's harmony.

Amid the flowers
He met her, and her garden's pleasant toil
Shared with a master's hand, for well he knew
The nature and the welfare of the plants
That most she prized. They loved the umbrageous trees,
And in their strong, columnar trunks beheld
The Almighty Architect, and for His sake
Paid them respect.

At the soft twilight hour,
He sate beside her silently, and watch'd
The pensive lustre of her lifted eye,
Intent to welcome the first star that hung
Its holy cresset forth. Unconsciously
Her moods of lonely musing stole away,
And his endear'd society became
Part of her being.

In her soul was nought
Of vanity, or coquetry to bar

That heaven-imparted sentiment which makes
All hope, all thought, all self, subordinate
Unto another's weal, while life shall last.

One morn, the orphan sought the private ear
Of her kind benefactress.
In low tones
With the sweet modesty of innocence,
She told that Conrad offered her his heart,
And in the tender confidence of trust
Entreated counsel from her changeless friend.

" Can you o'erlook the past, my Leonore ? "

"Our God forgives the penitent. And we
So prone to error, cannot we forgive?
The change in Conrad, months and years have made
More evident.
Might I but sooth away
The memory of his woes, and aid his feet
More steadfastly to tread in virtue's path,
And make him happier on his way to Heaven,
My life and love I'd gladly consecrate."

Wrapp'd in her arms the foster-mother gave
A tearful blessing, while on bended knee
Together they implored the approving smile
Of Him, who gives ability to make
And keep the covenant of unending love.

A rural bridal,
Cupid's ancient themes
Though more than twice-told, seem not wearisome
Or obsolete. The many tomes they prompt
Though quaint or prolix, still a place maintain
In library or boudoir, and seduce
The school-girl from her sleep, and lessons too.
But I no tint of romance have to throw
On this plain tale, or o'er the youthful pair
Who gladly took the irrevocable vow.

Their deep and thoughtful happiness required
No herald pomp. Buds of the snowy rose,
On brow and bosom, were the only gems
Of the young fair-hair'd bride, whose ringlets fell
Down to her shoulders:—nature's simple veil
Of wondrous grace.
A few true hearted friends
Witness'd the marriage-rite, with cheering smiles
And fervent blessings.
And the coming years
With all their tests of sunshine or of shade,
Belied no nuptial promise, striving each
With ardent emulation to surpass
Its predecessor in the heavenward path
Of duty and improvement.
Bertha's prayers
Were ever round them as a thread of gold
Wove daily in the warp and woof of life.

In their felicity she found her own
Reduplicated. In good deeds to all
Who sought her aid, or felt the sting of woe,
With unimpaired benevolence she wrought,
And tireless sympathy.
Ordain'd she seem'd
To show the beauty of the life that hath
God for its end.
Clearer its brightness gleam'd
As nearer to its heavenly goal it drew.
The smile staid with her till she went above,
Death harm'd it not. Her passport to that clime
Where Love begun on earth, doth end in joy,
Forevermore.

IN MEMORIAM.

REV. DR. T. M. COOLEY,

For more than sixty years Pastor of one Church in East Granville, Mass., died there in 1859, aged 83.

NOT in the pulpit where he joy'd to bear
The message of salvation, not beside
His study-lamp, nor in the fireside chair,
Encircled by those dearest ones who found
In him their life of life, nor in the homes
Of his beloved flock, sharing with them
All sympathies of sorrow or of joy,
Is seen the faithful Shepherd.
He hath gone
To yon blest Country where he long'd to be,
To stand before the Great White Throne, and join
That hymn of praise for which his course below
Gave preparation.
At one post he stood
From youth till fourscore years, averse to change
Though oft-times tempted. For he did not deem
Restless ambition or desire of gold

Fit counterpoise for that most sacred love
Born in the inner chambers of the soul,
And intertwining with a golden mesh
Pastor and people.

Like some lofty tree
Whose untransplanted roots in freshness meet
The living waters, and whose leaf is green
'Mid winter's gather'd frost, serene he stood,
More fondly honor'd for each added year,
While 'neath his shadow drew with reverent love
Successive generations.

Hoary Time
Linger'd with blessings for his latest day,
And now 'neath turf embalm'd with tears he sleeps,
Waiting the resurrection of the just.

MADAM OLIVIA PHELPS,

Widow of the late ANSON G. PHELPS, Esq., died at New York, April 24th, 1859, aged 74.

WHEN the good mother dieth, and the home
So long made happy by her boundless love
Is desolate and empty, there are tears
Of filial anguish, not to be represt;
And when the many friends who at her side
Sought social sympathy and counsel sweet,
Or the sad poor, who, for their Saviour's sake,
Found bountiful relief, and kind regard,
Stand at that altered threshold, and perceive
Faces of strangers from her casement look,
There is a pang not to be told in words.

Yet, when the christian, having well discharged
A life-long duty, riseth where no sin
Or possibility of pain or death
May follow, should there not be *praise* to Him
Who gives such victory?

Thus it is even now—
Tears with the triumph-strain;
For we are made
Of flesh as well as spirit, and are taught
By Joy and Sorrow, walking side by side,
And with strong contrast deepening truths divine.

But unto thee, dear friend, whose breath was prayer,
And o'er whose mortal sickness hovering Faith
Shed heaven's content, there was no further need
Of tutelage like that by which we learn,
Too slow, perchance, with vacillating minds,
What the disciples of our Lord should be;
For when the subjugation to God's will
Is perfect, and affliction all disarmed,
Is not life's lesson done?

MARTHA AGNES BONNER,

Child of ROBERT BONNER, Esq., died at New York, April 28th, 1859, aged 13 months.

THERE was a cradling lent us here,
To cheer our lot,
It was a cherub in disguise,
But yet our dim and earth-bow'd eyes
Perceiv'd it not.

Its voice was like the symphony
That lute-strings lend,
Yet tho' our hearts the music hail'd
As a sweet breath of heaven, they fail'd
To comprehend.

It linger'd till each season fill'd
Their perfect round,
The vernal bud, the summer-rose,
Autumnal gold, and wintry snows
Whitening the ground.

But when again reviving Spring
  Thro' flowers would roam,
And the white cherry blossoms stirr'd
Neath the soft wing of chirping bird,
A call from angel-harps was heard,
  "Cherub,—come home."

MADAM WHITING,

Widow of the late SPENCER WHITING, Esq., died at Hartford, April, 1859, aged 88.

LIFE'S work well done, how beautiful to rest.
Aye, lift your little ones to see her face,
So calmly smiling in its coffin-bed!
There is no wrinkle there,—no rigid gloom
To make them turn their tender glance away;
And when they say their simple prayer at night
With folded hands,—instruct their innocent lips
Meekly to say: "Our Father! may we live,
And die like her."

Her more than fourscore years
Chill'd not in her the genial flow of thought
Or energy of deed. The earnest power
To advance home-happiness, the kindly warmth
Of social intercourse, the sweet response
Of filial love, rejoicing in her joy,
And reverencing her saintly piety,
Were with her, unimpair'd, until the end.

A course like this, predicted close serene,
And so it was.

There came no cloud to dim
Her spirit's light, when at a beckoning brief
She heavenward went.

Miss'd is she here, and mourn'd;
From hall, from hearthstone, and from household board,
A beauty and a dignity have fled,—
And the heart's tears as freely flowed for her,
As for the loved ones, in their prime of days.
Age justly held in honor, hath a charm
Peculiarly its own, a symmetry
Of nearness to the skies.

And these were hers,
Whose life was duty, and whose death was peace.

DENISON OLMSTED, LL. D.,

Professor of Astronomy in Yale College, Conn., died at New Haven, May, 1859.

SPRING pour'd fresh beauty o'er the cultured grounds,
And woke to joyance every leaf and flower,
Where erst the Man of Science lov'd to find
Refreshment from his toils.

'Twas sweet to see
How Nature met him there, and took away
All weariness of knowledge. Yet he held
Higher communion than with fragrant shrub,
Or taper tree, that o'er the forest tower'd.
His talk was with the stars, as one by one,
Night, in her queenly regency, put forth
Their sprinkled gold upon her sable robe.
He knew their places, and pronounc'd their names,
And by their heavenly conversation sought
Acquaintance with their Maker.

Sang they not
Unto his uncloth'd spirit, as it pass'd
From sphere to sphere, above their highest ranks,
With its attendant angel?
We are dark.
We ask, and yet no answer.
But we trace
In clearest lines the shining course he took
Among life's duties, for so many years,
And hear those parting words, that "*all is peace!*"*
The harvest-song of true philosophy.

His epitaph is that which cannot yield
A mouldering motto to the tooth of time.
—Man works in marble, and it mocks his trust,
But the immortal mind doth ever keep
The earnest impress of the moulding hand,
And bear it onward to a race unborn.
—That is his monument.

---

* The last words of Professor Olmsted.

HERBERT FOSS,

Only son of SAMUEL S. FOSS, Esq., died May 23d, 1859, aged three years and three months.

"READ more, Papa," the loving infant cried,—
And meekly bow'd the listening ear, and fix'd
The ardent eye, devouring every word
Of his dear picture book. And then he spread
His arms, and folded thrice the father's neck.
—The mother came from church, and lull'd her boy
To quiet sleep, and laid him in his crib;
And as they watch'd the smile of innocence
That sometimes lightly floated o'er his brow
That Sabbath eve, they to each other said,
"*How beautiful.*"

There was another scene,—
The child lay compass'd round with Spring's white flowers,
Yet heav'd no breath to stir their lightest leaf.
And many a one who on that coffin look'd
And went their way, in tender whisper said
"*How beautiful!*"

Oh parents, ye who sit
Mourning for Herbert, in your empty room,
What if the darling of your fondest care
Scarce woke from his brief dream and went to Heaven?
—Our dream is longer, but 'tis mixed with tears.
For we are dreamers all, and only those
Fully awake, who dwell where naught deceives.

So, when time's vision o'er, you reach the land
Which hath no need of sun, or waning moon
To give it light, how sweet to hear your child
Bid you "*good morning*" with his cherub tongue.

His last words to his father, who was reading to him in a favorite book, were, "Read, more, papa, please read more." Soon after, and almost without warning, he died.

MRS. CHARLES N. CADWALLADER,

Died at Philadelphia, July 2nd, 1859, five weeks after her marriage.

THE year rolls round, and brings again
  The bright, auspicious day,
The marriage scene, the festive cheer,
  The group serenely gay,

The hopes that nurs'd by sun and shower
  O'er youth's fair trellis wound,
And in that consecrated rite
  Their full fruition found.

But One unseen amid the throng
  Drew near with purpose fell,
And lo! the orange-flowers were changed
  To mournful asphodel.

Five sabbaths walk'd the beautiful
  Her chosen lord beside,
But ere the sixth illumed the sky
  She was that dread One's bride.

Yet call her not the bride of Death
  Though in his bed she sleeps,
And broidering Myrtle richly green
  O'er her cold pillow creeps:

She hath a bower where angels dwell,
  A mansion with the blest,
For Jesus whom she trusted here,
  Receiv'd her to His rest.

REV. DR. JAMES W. ALEXANDER,

Pastor of the Fifth Avenue Church, New York, died at the Virginia Springs, July, 1859.

THE great and good. How startling is the knell
That tells he is but dust.
The echo comes
From where Virginia's health-reviving springs
Make many whole. But waiting there for him
The dark-winged angel who doth come but once,
Troubled the waters, and his latest breath
Fled, where his first was drawn.
That noble brow
So mark'd with intellect, so clear with truth,
Grave in its goodness, in its love serene,
Will it be seen no more?
That earnest voice
Filling the Temple-arch so gloriously,
With themes of import to the undying soul
Enforced by power of fervid eloquence
Is it forever mute?

That mind so rich
With varied learning and with classic lore,
Studious, progressive, affluent, profound,
That feeling heart, instinct with sympathy
For the world's family of grief and pain,
The dark in feature, or the lost in sin,
Say, are their treasures lost?
No, on the page
Of many a tome, traced by his tireless pen
They live and brighten for a race to come,
Prompting the wise, cheering the sorrowful,
And for the little children whom he loved
Meting out fitting words, like dewy pearls
Glittering along their path.
His chief delight
Was in his Master's work. How well performed
Speak ye whose feet upon Salvation's rock
Were planted through his prayers. His zeal involved
No element of self, but hand in hand
Walk'd with humility. He needeth not
Praise from our mortal lips. The monuments
Of bronze or marble, what are they to him
Who hath his firm abode above the stars?

—Yet may the people mourn, may freshly keep
The transcript of his life, nor wrongly ask
" When shall we look upon his like again ?"

MRS. JOSEPH MORGAN,

Died at Hartford, August, 1859.

I SAW her overlaid with many flowers,
Such as the gorgeous summer drapes in snow,
Stainless and fragrant as her memory.

Blent with their perfume came the pictur'd thought
Of her calm presence,—of her firm resolve
To bear each duty onward to its end,—
And of her power to make a home so fair,
That those who shared its sanctities deplore
The pattern lost forever.

Many a friend,
And none who won that title laid it down,
Muse on the tablet that she left behind,
Muse,—and give thanks to God for what she was,
And what she is;—for every pain hath fled
That with a barb'd and subtle weapon stood
Between the pilgrim and the promised Land.

But the deep anguish of the filial tear
We speak not of,—save with the sympathy
That wakes our own.
                                  And so, we bid farewell.

Life's sun at setting, may shed brighter rays
Than when it rose, and threescore years and ten
May wear a beauty that youth fails to reach:
The beauty of a fitness for the skies,—
Such nearness to the angels, that their song
"Peace and good will," like key-tone rules the soul,
And the pure reflex of their smile illumes
The meekly lifted brow.
                                  She taught us this,—
And then went home.

MISS ALICE BECKWITH,

Died at Hartford, September 23d, 1859.

THE beautiful hath fled
To join the spirit-train;
Earth interposed with strong array,
Love stretch'd his arms to bar her way,
All,—all in vain.

There was a bridal hope
Before her crown'd with flowers;
The orange blossoms took the hue
With which the cypress dank with dew
Darkeneth our bowers.

Affections strong and warm
Sprang round her gentle way,
Young Childhood, with a moisten'd eye,
And Friendship's tenderest sympathy
Watch'd her decay.

Disease around her couch
  Long held a tyrant sway,
Till vanished from her cheek, the rose,
And the fair flesh like vernal snows
  Wasted away.

Yet the dark Angel's touch
  Dissolv'd that dire control,
And where the love-knot cannot break
Nor pain nor grief intrusion make,
  Bore the sweet soul.

MARY SHIPMAN DEMING.

Died at Hartford, Nov. 11th, 1859, aged 4 years and 6 months.

THE garner'd Jewel of our heart,
The Darling of our tent!
Cold rains were falling thick and fast,
When forth from us she went.

The sweetest blossom on our tree,
When droop'd her fairy head,
We might not lay her 'mid the flowers,
For all the flowers were dead.

The youngest birdling of our nest,
Her song from us hath fled;
Yet mingles with a purer strain
That floats above our head.

We gaze,—her wings we may not see:
  We listen,—all in vain:
But when this wintry life is o'er,
  We'll hear her voice again.

REV. DR. F. W. HATCH,

Died at Sacramento, California, January 16th, 1860, aged 70.

A PLEASANT theme it is to think of him
That parted friend, whose noble heart and mind
Were ever active to the highest ends.
Even sceptics paid him homage 'mid their doubts,
Perceiving that his life made evident
A goodness not of earth.
His radiant brow
And the warm utterance of his lustrous eye
Told how the good of others triumph'd o'er
All narrowness of self. He deem'd it not
A worthy aim of Christ's true ministry
To chaffer for the gold that perisheth
Or waste its God-given powers on lifeless forms;
But love of souls, and love of Him who died
That they might live, gave impulse to his zeal.

— And so, while half a century chronicled
The change of empires, and the fall of kings

And death of generations like the leaves
That strew the forest 'neath autumnal skies,
He toil'd unswerving in that One Great Cause
To which the vigor of his youth was given.

—And as his life, its varied tasks well done
Shrouded its head and trustful went to Him
Who giveth rest and peace and rich reward
Unto his faithful servants, it behooves
Us to rejoice who have so long beheld
His pure example.
From it may we learn
Oh sainted Friend, wherever duty calls
With fervent hearts to seek for others' good,
And wear thy spirit-smile, and win even here
Some foretaste of the bliss that ne'er shall end.

MRS. PAYNE,

Wife of Right Rev. Bishop PAYNE, died at Monrovia, Liberia.

OH true and faithful! Twice ten earnest years
Of mission-toil in Afric's sultry clime
Attest thy patience in thy Master's cause,
Thy self-denial and humility.

Now, neath the shadow of the princely palm,
And where Liberia's church-crown'd summits rise,
Are sighs from sable bosoms, swelling deep
With gratitude for all thy hallow'd care.

—The Prelate, unto whom thy heart of hearts
Was link'd so tenderly,—who found in thee
Solace for exile from his native shore,
Laments thy loss, as the lone hours go by.
He mourns thee deepest, for he knew thee best,
Thy purity, thy sublimated search
For added holiness. With angel hand
Press thou thy pattern on us,—we who dwell
Amid the fullness of the bread from Heaven,
Forgetful of our heathen brother's need.

Now thou dost sweetly sleep, where pain and woe
Follow thee not. Their trial-time is o'er,
Their discipline perfected. For thy will
Was subjugated to the Will Divine,
And through a dear Redeemer's strength, thy soul
Hath won the victory.

MRS. MARY MILDENSTEIN ROBERTSON,

Wife of Rev. WILLIAM H. C. ROBERTSON, died at Magnolia, East Florida, January 13th, aged 34.

OUR buds have faded,—winter's frigid breath
Sigh'd o'er their bosoms, and they fell away,
So in these household bowers the ice of death
Bids rose and lily ere their prime decay,
And see a Passion-Flower from tropic skies
Beneath our drifted snows, not without requiem lies.

A brilliant daughter of the Cuban vales
Of generous mind, impulsive, strong and high
Twined the home-tendril where our northern gales
Sweep grove and forest with their minstrelsy,
Labor'd for classic lore with studious part,
And planted friendship's germ in many an answering heart.

Her filial piety intensely warm
Whose gushing tenderness no limit knew,

Clasp'd day and night, a Mother's wasted form
  And o'er her failing powers protection threw,
Cheering the darken'd soul with comfort sweet
And girding it anew, life's latest pang to meet.

Then came the sacred vow for good or ill,
  The life-long study of another's joy,
The raptur'd and unutterable thrill
  With which a mother greets her first-born boy,
The climax of those hopes and duties dear
Which Heaven's unerring hand accords to Woman's sphere.

And then the scene was ended, and she found
  What here her ardent nature vainly sought,
Unwithering flowers and music's tuneful sound
  Without a shadow or discordant thought,
And entered through a dear Redeemer's love
The never-changing clime of perfect rest above.

MADAM WILLIAMS,

Widow of the late EZEKIEL WILLIAMS, Esq., and Daughter of Chief Justice Oliver Ellsworth, died at Hartford, February 28th, 1860, aged 87.

SHE was a link that bound us to the past,—
To the great days of Washington, when men
Loving their country better than themselves
Show'd to the world what patriot virtue meant.
She on the knee of her majestic sire
Drew to her listening heart when life was new
Those principles that made his honored name
Synonymous with wisdom, and the might
Of holy truth.

So when in woman's sphere
She took her post of duty, still in all
The delicate proprieties of life,
The inner sanctities of household weal,
In social elegance, and in the deeds
That christian pity to the poor extends,
She was our model; and we saw in her
The perfect lady of the olden time.

Thus on the pleasant hill-top where she dwelt
In her green-terraced home, o'ercanopied
By graceful elm, mid evergreens and flowers,
The years stole over her, and slowly wrote
Their more than fourscore on her faded scroll,
While the kind care of unexhausted love
Guarded her long decline.

And now she sleeps
Where thro' the riven snows, the quickening turf
Gives emblem of the never-ending Spring,
That wraps the accepted soul in robes of joy.

SAMUEL G. OGDEN, ESQ.,

Died at Astoria, New York, April 5th, 1860.

UPON his suffering couch he lay,
  Whose noble form and mind
The stress of fourscore years had tried,
  Yet left a charm behind.
The charm of heaven-born happiness
  Whose beauty may not fade,
The charm of unimpair'd regard
  For all whom God had made.

Upon his suffering couch he lay,
  While sadly gathering there,
Were loved and loving ones, who made
  That honored life their care;
And 'mid the group, a daughter's voice
  Of wondrous sweetness read
Brief portions from the Book Divine,
  As his dictation led.

"Bow down thine ear, Most Merciful,
Oh, hearken while I speak,
Now in my time of utmost need,
To Thee alone I seek.
Shew me some token, Lord, for good,
Before I pass away,
For Thou hast ever been my strength,
My comforter and stay." *

So when that precious breath went forth,
Her gentle hand was laid
To close those pale and trembling lids
In slumber's dreamless shade,
And then, the pure and sacred flowers
She for his burial twined,
And bade her struggling grief be still
Till the last rite declined.

Through every trial change of life
Had reign'd within her breast
A holy zeal of filial love,
That could not be represt;
Its memories, like a music strain,
Still in that casket swell,
And wake perchance, some fond response
Where watching angels dwell.

---

* The 86th Psalm, one of his favorites, as death drew nigh was often read to him by his daughter, who never left him, day or night, during his sickness, and "out of whose arms," says one who was present, "when he drew his last breath, the angels took him."

MR. GEORGE BEACH,

Died at Hartford, May 4th, 1860.

AYE, robe yourselves in black, light messengers
Whose letter'd faces to the people tell
The pulse and pressure of the passing hour.
'Tis fitting ye should sympathize with them,
And tint your tablets with a sable hue
Who bring them tidings of a loss so great.

What have they lost?
An upright man, who scorn'd
All subterfuge, who faithful to his trust
Guarded the interests they so highly prized,
With power and zeal unchang'd, from youth to age.

Yet there's a sadder sound of bursting tears
From woe-worn helpless ones, from widow'd forms
O'er whom he threw a shelter, for his name
Long mingled with their prayers, both night and morn.

The Missionary toward the setting sun
Will miss his liberal hand that threw so wide
Its secret alms. The sons of want will miss
His noble presence moving thro' our streets
Intent on generous deeds; and in the Church
He loved so well, a silence and a chasm
Are where the fervent and responsive voice,
And kingly beauty of the hoary head
So long maintained their place.
                                        Sudden he sank,
Though not unwarn'd.
                                        A chosen band had kept
Watch through the night, and earnest love took note
Of every breath. But when approaching dawn
Kindled the east, and from the trees that bowered
His beautiful abode, awakening birds
Sent up their earliest carol, he went forth
To meet the glories of the unsetting sun,
And hear with unseal'd ear the song of heaven.

—So they who truest loved and deepest mourn'd,
Had highest call to praise, for best they knew
The soul that had gone home unto its God.

MISS MARGARET C. BROWN,

Died at Hartford, May 12th, 1860.

GONE, pure in heart! unto thy fitting home,
Where nought of ill can follow. O'er thy life
There swept no stain, and o'er its placid close
No shadow.
As for us, who saw thee move
From childhood onward, loving and serene,
To every duty faithful, we who feel
The bias toward self too often make
Our course unequal, or beset with thorns,
Give thanks to Him, the Giver of all good,
For what thou wert, but most for what thou art.

Thy meek and reverent nature cheer'd the heart
Of hoary Age even in thine early bloom,
And with sweet tenderness of filial care,
And perfect sympathy, thy shielding arm
Pillow'd a Mother's head, till life went out.

We yield thee back, with sound of holy hymns,
Flowers in thy hand, and bosom,—parting gifts
Of Spring, that makes our earth so beautiful,
Faintly prefiguring thine eternal gain
Of flowers that never fade and skies that need
Not sun nor moon to light them.
                              So farewell,
Our grief is selfish, yet it hath its way,
Nor can we stand beside thine open grave
Without a tear.
                              Yet still doth chasten'd faith
Ask help of God, to render back with praise
A soul to which He gave the victory.

MISS FRANCES WYMAN TRACY,

Adopted daughter of Mrs. WILLIAM TRACY, died at New York, in 1860, aged 17.

O YOUNG and beautiful, thy step
  Was light with fairy grace,
And well the music of thy voice
  Accorded with thy face,

And blent with those attractive charms
  How fair it was to see
Thy tenderness for her who fill'd
  A Mother's place to thee.

Yet all the pure and holy ties
  Thus round thy being wove,
They are not lost, they are not dead,
  They have a life above.

What though the sleepless care of love
   Might not avail to save,
And sorrow with her dropping tear
   Keeps vigil o'er thy grave,

Faith hath a rainbow for the cloud,
   A solace for the pain,
A promise from the Book Divine
   To rise, nor part again.

DEACON NORMAND SMITH,

Died at Hartford, May 22d, 1860, aged 87.

One saintly man the less, to teach us how
Wisely to live,—one blest example more
To teach us how to die.
Fourscore and seven,
Swept not the beauty of his brow away,
Nor quell'd his voice of music, nor impair'd
The social feeling that through all his life
Ran like a thread of gold.
In filial arms
Close wrapp'd with watchful tenderness, he trod
Jordan's cold brink.
The world was beautiful,
But Christ's dear love so wrought within his heart
That to depart seem'd better.
Many a year
He lent his influence to the church he loved,
For unity and peace, and countless gems
Dropp'd from his lips when the last sickness came,

To fortify young pilgrims in the course
That leads to glory and eternal life.

As the frail flesh grew weak, the soul look'd forth
With added brightness thro' the clear, dark eye,
As though it saw unutterable things,
Or heard the welcome of beloved ones
Who went to rest before him.
So, with smiles,
And prayers and holy hymns, and loving words
He laid the burden of the body down,
And slept in Jesus.

MRS. HELEN TYLER BEACH,

Wife of Mr. C. N. BEACH, died at Philadelphia, July 30th, 1860.

How strange that One who yesterday
   Shed radiance round her sphere,
Thus, in the prime of life and health,
   Should slumber on the bier.

How sad that One who cheer'd her home
   With love's unvarying grace,
Should leave at hearth-stone and at board
   Nought save a vacant place.

The beaming hope that bright and fair
   Around her cradle shone,
Made cloudless progress year by year,
   With lustre all its own,

While still unselfish and serene
   Her daily course she drew,
To every generous impulse warm
   To every duty true:

Yet all these pure and hallowed charms
   To favor'd mortals given,
That make their loss to earth so great,
   Enhance the gain of Heaven.

MRS. ELIZABETH HARRIS,

Died at Hartford, Sunday evening, September 9th, 1860, aged 80.

OH sorrowing Daughter, left alone
In home's deserted sphere,
Where every object group'd around,
In pleasant room, or garden's bound
Is twined by links of sight or sound
With the lost Mother dear;

Yet take sweet thoughts thy grief to soothe
Of what she was below,
Her years to faithful duty given,
Her comfort in the Book of Heaven,
Her ready trust when life was riven,
To Christ, her Lord, to go.

And take sweet memories of the care
That smoothed her couch of pain,
The grateful love that o'er her way
Kept tender vigil, night and day,
And let its pure, reflected ray
Thy drooping heart sustain.

So shall thy faith the pang assuage
  That heaves thy mourning breast;
For nearer brings each setting sun
Their blessed meeting who have won
The plaudit of the Judge, "Well done,
  Come, enter to my rest."

MISS ANNA M. SEYMOUR,

Died at Hartford, August 24th, 1860.

THE beauteous brow, the form of grace,
With all their youthful charms,
The hand that woke the pencil's power,
And bore to penury's lowly bower,
The never-wearied alms,

The sweet, sweet voice that duly cheer'd
A grateful Sabbath train,
The uprais'd eye that taught them more
Of Heaven, than all their student lore,
Must ne'er return again.

She took her flight as from the cage
Enfranchised warblers glide,
Though friends were dear, and life was fair,
She saw her Saviour standing there,
Beyond rough Jordan's tide.

Praise, praise to Him, whose faithful hand
  Prepared her glorious place,
For us is loss,—for her release,
The robe of rest, the home of peace,—
  For us, the pilgrim race.

Praise,—praise for her,—though love and grief
  Still mournful vigil kept,—
The tear-wet incense He will take
Who at the grave, for friendship's sake,
  In holy sadness wept.

CALEB HAZEN TALCOTT,

Son of C. TALCOTT, Esq., died at Hartford, October 26th, 1860, aged 2 years and 6 months.

THERE came a merry voice
  Forth from those lips of rose,
As tireless through its fringing flowers
  The tuneful brooklet flows,

And with the nurslings feet
  Engaged in busy play
It made the parents' pleasant home
  A joyance all the day.

There breath'd a languid tone
  Forth from those pallid lips,
As when some planet of the night
  Sinks in its dread eclipse.

" Sing to me, sing," it cried,
  While the red fever reign'd,
" Oh sing of Jesus,"* it implored
  While struggling life remained.

Then rose a mournful sound,
  The solemn funeral knell,
And silent anguish settled where
  The nursery's idol fell.

But he who so desired
  His Saviour's name to hear
Doth in His glorious presence smile,
  Above this cloud-wrapp'd sphere.

---

* His request, during his sickness was, " Sing to me of Jesus."

MISS JANE PENELOPE WHITING,

Died at Portland, Connecticut, January 1st, 1861.

I THINK of her unfolding prime,
Her childhood bright and fair,
The speaking eye, the earnest smile,
The dark and lustrous hair,

The fondness by a Mother's side
To cling with docile mind,
Fast in the only sister's hand
Her own forever twined,

The candor of her trustful youth,
The heart that freshly wove
Sweet garlands even from thorn-clad bowers,
Because it dwelt in love,

The stainless life, whose truth and grace
Made each beholder see
The gladness of a spirit tuned
To heavenly harmony.

But when this fair New-Year looked forth
   Over the old one's grave,
While bridal pleasures neath her roof
   Their bright infusion gave,

Upon the lightning's wing there came
   A message none might stay,
An angel,—standing at her side.
   To bear the soul away.

For us, was sorrow's startling shock,
   The tear, the loss, the pain,
For her, the uncomputed bliss
   Of never-ending gain.

MISS ANNA FREEMAN,

Died at Mansfield, Connecticut, February, 1861.

THE world seems drearier when the good depart,
The just, the truthful, such as never made
Self their chief aim, nor strove with glozing words
To counterfeit a love they never felt;
But steadfast and serene—to Friendship gave
Its sacred scope, and ne'er from Duty shrank,
Though sternest toil and care environ it.
These, loving others better than themselves,
Fulfill the gospel rule, and taste a bliss
While here below, unknown to selfish souls,
And when they die, must find the clime where dwells
A God of truth, as tend the kindred streams
To their absorbing ocean.
Such was she
Who left us yesterday. Her speaking smile
Her earnest footstep hastening to give aid
Or sympathy, her ready hand well-skill'd

In all that appertains to Woman's sphere,
Her large heart pouring life o'er every deed,
And her warm interchange of social joy
Stay with us as a picture.
                                    There, we oft
Musing, shall contemplate each lineament
With mournful tenderness, through gushing tears,
That tell our loss, and her unmeasured gain.

MADAM POND,

Widow of the late Caleb Pond, Esq., died at Hartford, February 19th 1861, aged 73.

Would any think who marked the smile
On yon untroubled face,
That threescore years and ten had fled
Without a wrinkling trace?

Yet age doth sometimes skill to guard
The beauty of its prime,
And hold a quenchless lamp above
The water-floods of time.

And she, for whom we mourn, maintained
Through every change and care,
Those hallowed virtues of the soul
That keep the features fair.

They raised a little child to look
Into the coffin deep,
Who dream'd the lovely lady lay
But in a transient sleep,

And gazed upon the face of death
With eye of tranquil ray,
Well pleased, as with the snowy flowers,
That on her bosom lay.

Then on the sad procession moved,
And mid funereal gloom,
The only son was there to lay
His mother in the tomb.

Oh, memories of an only child,
How strong and rich ye are!
A wealth of concentrated love
That none beside can share.

And hence, the filial grief that swells,
When breaks its latest tie,
Flows onward with a fuller tide
Than meets the common eye.

With voice of holy prayer she pass'd
Forth from her pleasant door,
Where tender recollections dwell
Though she returns no more.

Even so the pure and pious rise
From tents of pain and woe,
But leave a precious transcript here
To guide us where they go.

ANNIE SEYMOUR ROBINSON,

Daughter of Lucius F. Robinson and Mrs. Eliza S. Robinson, died at Hartford, Wednesday, April 10th, 1861, aged 6 years and 2 months.

Dids't hear him call, my beautiful ?—
The Sire, so fond and dear
Who ere the last moon's waning ray,
Pass'd in his prime of days away,
And hath not left his peer ?

Say, beckoning from yon silver cloud
Though none beside might see,
A hand that erst with love and pride
Its little daughter's steps would guide—
Stretch'd out that hand for thee ?

The wreathing buds of snowy rose
That o'er thy bosom lay,
Were symbols in their beauty pale,
Of thy young life so sweet and frail,
And all unstain'd as they.

Oh stricken hearts!—bear up,—bear on,—
  Think of your Saviour's grace,
Think of the spirit-welcome given,
When at the pearly gate of Heaven,
  Father and child embrace.

MRS. GEORGIANA IVES COMSTOCK,

Died at Hartford, April 30th, 1861, aged 22.

I SAW a brilliant bridal.
All that cheers
And charms the leaping heart of youth was there;
And she, the central object of the group,
The cherished song-bird of her father's house,
Array'd in beauty, was the loved of all.
Would I could tell you what a world of flowers
Were concentrated there—how they o'erflow'd
In wreaths and clusters—how they climb'd and swept
From vase to ceiling, with their gay festoons
Whispering each other in their mystic lore
Of fragrance, and consulting how to swell,
As best they might, the tide of happiness.

A few brief moons departed and I sought
The same abode. There was a gather'd throng
Beyond the threshold stone. A few white flowers
Crept o'er a bosom and a gentle hand

That clasp'd them not. A holy hymn awoke
In plaintive melody; but she who breath'd
The very soul of music from her birth,
Lay there with close-seal'd lips.
                              And the same voice
That in the flushing of the autumnal rose
Gladly pronounced the irrevocable words
"*What God hath join'd together let no man*
Asunder put," now, in the chasten'd tones
Of deep humility and tenderness,
Strove, from the armory of Heaven, to gird
The hearts that freshly bled.

                              At close of day,
In the lone, sadden'd hour of musing thought,
I seem'd to view a scene where, side by side,
Bridals and burials gleam'd—the smile and tear—
Anguish and joy—peace in her heavenly vest,
And brazen-throated war—and heard a cry,
"Such is man's life below."
                              I would have wept,
Save that a symphony of harps unseen
Broke from a hovering cloud; "Lo! we are they
Who from earth's tribulation rose and found
Our robes made white. Henceforth we grieve no more."

List! List! She mingleth in that raptur'd strain
Who said so sweetly to her spirit's-guide,
That the dear Lord whom she had early serv'd

Stood near in her extremity, and gave
Her soul full willingness to leave a world
All bright with beauty, and requited love.

And so Death lost his victory, tho' he snatched
The unwither'd garland out of Hymen's hand,
And wound it in cold mockery round the tomb.

WENTWORTH ALEXANDER,

Son of Dr. WILLIAM and Mrs. MARY WENTWORTH ALEXANDER, died at Fayette, Iowa, May, 1861, aged 2 years.

Coming in from play, he laid his head on his mother's bosom, and said "Mama, "*take your boy,—boy tired*," and never looked up healthfully again.

BOY tired! the drooping infant said,
And meekly laid his noble head,
  Down on that shielding breast,
Which mid all change of grief, or wo,
Had been his Paradise below,
  His comforter and rest.

Boy tired! Alas for nursing Love,
That sleepless toiled and watched and strove,
  For dire disease portends.
Alas for Science and its skill
Opposed to his unpitying will
  This mortal span that rends.

Boy tired! So thou hast past away,
From heat and burden of the day,
  From snares that manhood knows,—
From want and wo and deadly strife,
From wrong, and weariness of life,
  Hast found serene repose.

Boy tired! Those words of parting pain
Thou never more wilt breathe again,
  Nor lift the moaning cry,
For naught to wound or vex, or cloy,
Invades the cherub home of joy,
  No shade obscures the sky.

O, mother! When above ye meet,
When all these years, so few and fleet,
  Fade like a mist away,
This sorrow that thy soul hath bowed,
Shall seem but as an April cloud,
  Before the noon-tide ray.

MRS. HARVEY SEYMOUR,

Died at Hartford, Sunday, May 5th, 1861.

SHE found a painless avenue to make
The great transition from a world of care
To one of rest.
It was the Sabbath day,
And beautiful with smile of vernal sun
And the up-springing fragrance from the earth,
With all that soothing quietude which links
The consecrated season unto Him
Who bade the creatures He had made, revere
And keep it holy.
From her fair abode,
Lovely with early flowers, she took her way
The second time, unto the House of God,
And side by side with her life's chosen friend
Walk'd cheerfully. Within those hallow'd courts,
Where holds the soul communion with its God,
She listening sate.

But then she lean'd her head
Upon her husband's shoulder, and unmark'd
By one distorted feature, by the loss
Or blanching of the rose-tint on her cheek,
Rose to more perfect worship.
It might seem
As if a sacred temple, purified
By prayers and praises, were a place sublime,
Of fitting sanctity, wherein to hear
The inexpressive call that summoneth
The ready spirit upward.
But the change
In her delightful home, what words can tell!
The shock and contrast, when a mind so skill'd
With order and efficiency to fill
Each post of woman's duty and of love,
Vanished from all its daily ministries,
And the lone daughter found the guiding voice
Silent forevermore.
Her's was the heart
For an unswerving friendship, warm and true,
And self-forgetful; her's the liberal hand
To those who pine in cells of poverty,
The knowledge of their state, the will to aid,
The thought that cared for them, the zeal that blest.

Hence, tears o'er rugged cheeks fell fast for her,
And the old white-hair'd pensioner knelt down
Beside her lifeless clay and cross'd himself,

And pour'd his desolate prayer; for her kind heart
Saw in the creed of varying sects no bar
To charity, but in their time of need
Held all as brethren.

'Twas a pleasant spot,
Amid fresh verdure, where they laid her down,
While the young plants that o'er a daughter's grave
Took summer-rooting seemed in haste to reach
Forth their incipient roots and tendrils green
To broider her turf-pillow.

Sleep in peace,
Ye, whom the ties of nature closely bound,
And death disparted for a little while,
Mother and gentle daughter, sleep in peace;
Your forms engraven deep on loving hearts,
As with a diamond's point, till memory fade.

MRS. FREDERICK TYLER,

Died at Hartford, Wednesday, June 19th, 1861.

THEY multiply above, with whom we walk'd
In tender friendship, and whose steadfast step,
Onward and upward, was a guide to us
In duty's path.

They multiply above,
Making the mansions that our Lord prepared
And promised His redeemed, more beautiful
To us, the wayside pilgrims.

One, this day
Hath gone, whose memory like a loving smile
Lingereth behind her. She was skilled to charm
And make her pleasant home a cloudless scene
Of happiness to children and to guests;
But most to him whose heart for many years
Did safely trust in her, finding his cares
Divided and his pleasures purified.

A sweet-voiced kindness, prompting word and deed,
Dwelt ever with her; and, when hours of pain
Narrowed the scope of her activities,
Its radiance comforted the friends who came
To comfort her.

With soul serenely calm
She felt the cherished ties of earth recede
That long had bound her in such fond control,
And with a hymn upon her whitening lip,
A thrilling cadence tremulously sweet,
Into the valley of the shade of death
Entered unshrinkingly.

How blest to rise
With song of praise, unto that tuneful choir
Whose harps are ne'er unstrung, and have no tone
Of weary dissonance.

The rose of June
Was in its flushing, and a few brief moons
Had cast upon her lovely daughter's grave
Their hallowed lustre, when we laid so low
Her perishable part, seeming to hear
Their chant of welcome, unto whom the Sun
No more goes down, and partings are unknown.

MISS LAURA KINGSBURY,

Died at Hartford, July, 1861.

FAITHFUL and true in duty's sacred sphere,
  How like the summer-lightning hath she fled!
One moment bending o'er the letter'd page,—
  The next reposing with the silent dead.

No more by shaded lamp, or garden fair;—
  Yet hath she left a living transcript here,
Yon helpless orphans will remember her,*
  And the young invalid she skilled to cheer;

And he who trusted in her from his birth,
  As to a Mother's love,—and friends who saw
Her goodness seeking no applause from earth,
  But ever steadfast to its heavenly law:

For she, like her of old, with listening ear
Sate at the Saviour's feet and won His plaudit dear.

---

*She was a judicious and faithful manager of the Female Beneficent Society of Hartford.

GOVERNOR JOSEPH TRUMBULL,

Died at Hartford, August 4th, 1861; and his wife, Mrs. ELIZA STORRS TRUMBULL, the night after his funeral.

DEATH'S shafts fly thick, and love a noble mark.
—And one hath fallen who bore upon his shield
The name and lineage of an honor'd race
Who gave us rulers in those ancient days
Where truth stood first and gain was left behind.

—His was the type of character that makes
Republics strong,—unstain'd fidelity,—
A dignity of mind that mark'd unmov'd
The unsought honors clustering round his path,
And chang'd them into duties. With firm step
On the high places of the earth he walk'd,
Serving his Country, not to share her spoils,
Nor pamper with exciting eloquence
A parasite ambition.
With clear eye
And cautious speech, and judgment never warp'd

By fancy or enthusiasm, he pursued
An even, upright course. His bounties sought
Unostentatious channels, and he loved
To help the young who strove to help themselves,
Aiding their oar against opposing tides,
Into the smooth, broad waters.
Thus flow'd on
His almost fourscore years,—levying slight tax
On form or mind, while self-forgetful still,
He rose to prop the sad, or gird the weak.

—Yet, when at last, in deep repose he lay,
His classic features, and unfurrow'd brow,
Wearing the symmetry of earlier days
Which Death, as if relenting, render'd back
In transitory gleam, 'twas sweet to hear
His aged Pastor at the coffin-side
Bearing full tribute to his piety
So many lustrums,that consistent faith
Which nerv'd his journey and had led him home.
Home?—Yes! Give thanks, ye, who still travel on,
Oft startled, as some pilgrim from your side
Falls through the arches of Time's broken bridge
Without a warning, and is seen no more—
Give thanks that he is safe,—at home,—in heaven.

Back to the grave, from whence ye scarce have turn'd,
Break up the clods on which the dews of night

But twice had rested. Lo! another comes.
She, who for many years had garner'd up
Her heart's chief strength in him, finding his love
Armor and solace, in all weal or woe,
Seem'd the world poor without him, that she made
Such haste to join him in the spirit-land?
Through the dark valley of the shade of death,
Treading so close behind him? Scarce his lip
Learn'd the new song of heaven, before she rose
To join the enraptur'd strain. Her earthly term
Of fair and faithful duty well perform'd,
In fear of God, and true good will to man,
How blessed thus to enter perfect rest,
Where is no shadow of infirmity,
Nor fear of change, but happy souls unite
In high ascriptions to redeeming Love.

And thou,* sole daughter of their house and heart,
Leading thy mournful little ones to look
Into the open and insatiate tomb,
With what a rushing tide thy sorrows came.
—The sudden smiting, in his glorious prime
Of him who held the key of all thy joys,—
The fair child following him,—the noble Friend
Who watch'd thee with parental pride,—and now
Father and Mother have forsaken thee.
—The lessons of a life-long pilgrimage
Thou hast achiev'd, while yet a few brief moons

With waning finger, as in mockery wrote
Of treasur'd hopes, more fleeting than their own.

—But mays't thou from these sterner teachings gain
A higher seat, where no o'ershadowing cloud
Veileth the purpose of God's discipline.
And mid their glad embrace,—the gone before,—
The re-united ne'er to part,—behold
The teaching of no bitter precept lost,
Nor tear-sown seed fail of its harvest crown.

---

* Mrs. Eliza S. Robinson, the only child of Governor and Mrs. Trumbull, whose early life had been a scene of singularly unbroken felicity, was appointed to a fearful contrast of rapid and severe bereavements. Her noble husband, Lucius F. Robinson, Esq., in the midst of his days and usefulness, was suddenly smitten,—immediately after, their beautiful child, Annie Seymour,—then her distinguished relative, Chief Justice Storrs, who from her birth had regarded her with a fatherly love; and then both her parents, side by side, almost hand in hand, passed to the tomb.

With unsurpassed calmness, she met this whelming tide of sorrow, girding herself to her maternal duties, in the armor of a disciple of Jesus Christ. Yet with little warning, she was herself soon summoned to follow those beloved ones, dying in August, 1862, at the age of 35, leaving three orphan daughters, and a large circle of friends to lament the loss of her beautiful example of every christian grace and virtue.

MRS. EMILY ELLSWORTH,

Wife of Govenor ELLSWORTH, and daughter of Noah Webster, LL. D., died at Hartford, August 23d, 1861.

NOT with the common forms of funeral grief
We mourn for her who in the tomb this day
Taketh her narrow couch. For we have need
Of such example as she set us here,
The sphere of christian duty beautified
By gifts of intellect, and taste refined;
A precious picture, set in frame of gold
And hung on high.

Hers was a life that bore
The test of scrutiny, and they who saw
Its inner ministration, day by day,
Bore fullest witness to its symmetry,
Its delicate tissues, and unwavering crown
Of piety. A heritage of fame,
And the rich culture of her early years
Wrought no contempt for woman's household care,
But gave it dignity. Order was hers,
And system, and an industry that weighed

The priceless value of each fleeting hour.
Hers was a charm of manner felt by all,
A reference for authorities that marked
The olden time, and that true courtesy
Which made the aged happy.

Scarce it seemed
That she was of their number, or the links
Of threescore years and ten, indeed had wound
Their coil around her, with such warmth the heart,
And cloudless mind retained their energies.
Beauty and grace were with her to the last,
And fascination that withheld the guest
Beyond the allotted time.
More would we say,
But her affections 'tis not ours to touch
In lays so weak. He of their worth might tell,
Whose dearest hopes so long with hers entwined,
And they who shared the intense maternal love,
That knew no pause of effort, no decay,
No weariness, but glazed the dying eye
With heaven-born lustre.

So, we bid farewell;
Friend and Exemplar, we who tread so close
In thine unechoing footsteps.

Be thy faith
As strong for us, when we the bridge shall pass
To the grand portal of Eternity.

REV. STEPHEN JEWITT, D. D.,

Died at New Haven, August 25th, 1861, aged 78.

I WELL remember him, and heard his voice
In vigorous prime, beneath the Temple-Arch,
His brow enkindling with its holy themes.

And I remember to have heard it said
In what a patient studiousness of toil
His youth had pass'd, and how his manhood's tent
Spread out its curtains joyously, to shield
His aged parents, from their lonely home
Amid the glory of the Berkshire hills,
Turning in tender confidence to him;
And giving scope to earn the boon that crowns
The fifth commandment of the decalogue.
—And this he did, for their departing prayer
Fell balmily upon his filial heart,
As when the dying Jacob, blessed his race
And worshipp'd, leaning on his patriarch-staff.

—His lengthened life amid a peaceful scene
Flow'd on, with loving memories.
He had serv'd
The Church he lov'd, not in luxurious ease,
But self-forgetful as a pioneer,
When she had fewer sons to build her walls,
Or teach her gates salvation.
And the dome
Of yon fair College on its classic heighth
So beautiful without, and blest within,—
By liberal deeds, as well as gracious words
Remembereth him and with recording pen
Upon the tablet of its earliest* friends
Engraves his name.
So, full of honor'd years,
Blessing and blest, he took his way, above.

* The Rev. Dr. Jewitt was the first founder of a scholarship in Trinity College, Hartford, a quarter of a century since.

MISS DELIA WOODRUFF GODDING,

A faithful Teacher of the young from early years, and recently the Principal of a Female Seminary and Boarding School at St. Anthony, Minnesota, died suddenly of an attack of fever, while on a visit at her paternal home in Vermont, September, 15th, 1861.

THINE earnest life is over, sainted Friend!
And hush'd the teaching voice that gladly pour'd
Knowledge and goodness o'er the plastic mind.
—Full many a pupil of thy varied lore
Amid thine own New-England's elm-crowned vales
Holds thee in tenderness of grateful thought,
And far away in the broad-featured west
Where the strong Sire of waters robes in green
The shores of Minnesota, comes a wail
From youthful bands expecting thy return,
To guide them, as the shepherd leads the lamb.

They watch in vain.
The pleasant halls are dark
Once lighted by thy smile, and flowing tears
Reveal the love that linger'd there for thee.

Said we thy life was o'er?
Forgive the words.
We take them back.
Thou hast begun to live.
Here was the budding, there the perfect flower,
Here the faint star, and there the unsetting sun,
Here the scant preface, there the open Book
Where angels read forever.

Here on the threshold, the dim vestibule
Thou with a faithful hand didst toil to tune
That harp of praise within the unfolding heart
Which 'neath the temple-arch not made with hands
Swells the full anthem of Eternity.

MISS SARA K. TAYLOR,

Died at Hartford, October 23d, 1861, aged 20.

How beautiful in death
The young and lovely sleeper lies—
Sweet calmness on the close-sealed eyes,
Flowers o'er the snowy neck and brow
Where lustrous curls profusely flow;
If 'twere not for the icy chill
That from her marble hand doth thrill,
And for her lip that gives no sound,
And for the weeping all around,
How beautiful were death.

How beautiful in life!
Her pure affections heavenward moving,
Her guileless heart so full of loving,
Her joyous smile, her form of grace,
Her clear mind lighting up the face,
And making home a blessed place,
Still breathing thro' the parents' heart
A gladness words could ne'er impart,
A faith that foil'd affliction's dart—
How beautiful her life.

Gone to the Better Land!
Before the world's cold mist could shade
The brightness on her spirit laid,
Before the autumnal breeze might fray
One leaflet from her wreath away,
Or crisp one tendril of the vine
That hope and happiness did twine—
Gone—in the soul's unfaded bloom
That dreads no darkness of the tomb—
Gone to the Better Land.

MR. JOHN WARBURTON,

Died at Hartford, November, 1861.

THE knot of crape upon yon stately door,
And sadness brooding o'er the sun-bright halls,
What do they signify?
                                Death hath been there
Where truth and goodness hand in hand with love
Walk'd for so many years.
                                Death hath been there,
To do mid flowing tears his mighty work,
Extinguishing the tyranny of pain
And taking the immortal essence home
Where it would be.
                                Yet is there left behind
A transcript that we cherish, and a chasm
We have no power to fill. Almost it seems
That we beheld him still, with quiet step
Moving among us, saintly and serene,
Clear-sighted, upright, held in high regard,
Yet meekly unambitious, seeking nought

Of windy honor from the mouth of men
But with the Gospel's perfect code content,
Breathing good-will to all.
Freely his wealth
Wrought blessed channels mid the sons of need,
Lending Philanthropy and Piety
A stronger impulse in their mission-course
To ameliorate and save.

So, thus intent
On higher deeds and aims than earth supplies,
An adept in that true philosophy
Learnt only in Christ's school, he calmly went
Unto his Master and the Class above.

REV. HENRY ALBERTSON POST,

Died at Warrensburgh, New York, November 12th, 1861, aged 26.

*READ me rejoicing Psalms,
  Oh dearest one, and best!
I go from war to peace,
  From pain to glorious rest,

Where the bright life-tree sheds
  Around its precious balms,
So, while I linger here
  Read me rejoicing psalms.

And when my place I take
  Amid the ransom'd throng
Who through a Saviour's love
  Uplift the immortal song,

Repress the tear of grief
  That washes faith away,
And brave in zeal and love
  Await our meeting-day.

Yes, let thy course below
   Through all its fleeting days
In its angelic ministries
   Be as a psalm of praise.

---

* His request of his wife during the sufferings of an acute dyptheria, which suddenly separated him from an attached people, was, "Read me rejoicing Psalms."

MISS CAROLINE L. GRIFFIN,

Died at New York, November 17th, 1861.

WRITTEN ON HER BIRTH-DAY.

THE day returns, beloved friend
  When in thy Mother's arms
Thou a fair gift from Heaven wert laid
  In all thine infant charms,
That day, with cloudless sky returns,
  But yet thou art not here
And from the smitten Mother's eye
  Distils the mourner's tear.

The wondrous brightness of thy smile,
  Thy tones of greeting kind,
The love of knowledge that inspired
  Thy strong and ardent mind,
Thy pity for the suffering poor,
  Thy patient zeal to teach
Their children, though in manners rude
  And ignorant in speech,

And all thy many deeds and words
  Of friendship's earnest part,
Are with a never-fading trace
  Depictured on my heart.
But thou art with that Saviour dear
  Who was thine early choice,
And mid thy blooming youth didst bend
  A listener to His voice,

So thy firm faith without a fear
  Launch'd forth on Jordan's wave
The victor-palm-branch in thy hand
  That o'er stern Death He gave;
And may we meet, beloved friend
  At God's appointed day
Where every care and pain of earth
  Have fled like dreams away.

MR. NORMAND BURR,

Editor of the "Christian Secretary" for more than twenty years, died at Hartford, December 5th, aged 59.

WE knew him as a man of sterling worth,
Whose good example is a legacy
Better than gold for those he leaves behind.

—His inborn piety flowed forth in streams
Of social kindness and domestic love,
Cheering with filial warmth the parents' heart,
And making his own home a pleasant place.

—His was that self-reliant industry,
Smiling at hardship, which develops well
The energies of manhood, and lends strength
To commonwealths.

By silent messenger,
A weekly scroll, he strove to spread abroad
The stores of knowledge, and increase the fruits
Of righteousness. Hence is his loss bemoan'd
By many who had never seen his face
Here in the flesh, but thro' the links of thought
Held intimate communion.

The true life
Of virtue, is not lost to men below,
Though smitten by the frost of death it fall,—
Its quickening memory survives, to gird
On in the heavenward race, and gently guide
Where the high plaudit of the Judge is won.

HON. THOMAS S. WILLIAMS,

Late Chief Justice of Connecticut, died at Hartford, on Sunday **morning,** December 15th, 1861, aged 84.

'TIS not for pen and ink,
Or the weak measures of the muse, to give
Fit transcript of his virtues who hath risen
Up from our midst this day.

And yet 'twere sad
If such example were allow'd to fleet
Without abiding trace for those behind.
To stand on earth's high places, in the garb
Of Christian meekness, yet to comprehend
And track the tortuous policies of guile
With upright aim, and heart immaculate,
To pass just sentence on the wiles of fraud,
And deeds of wickedness, yet freshly keep
The fountain of good-will to all mankind,
To mark for more than fourscore years, a line
Of light without a mist, are victories
Not oft achiev'd by frail humanity,
Yet were they his.

Of charities that knew
No stint or boundary, save the woes of man
He wish'd no mention made. But doubt ye not
Their record is above.
Without the tax
That age doth levy, on the eye or ear,
Movement of limbs, or social sympathies,
In sweet retirement of domestic joy
His calm, unshadow'd pilgrimage was closed
By an unsighing transit.

Our first wintry morn
Lifted its Sabbath face, and saw him sit
All reverent, at the table of his Lord,
And heard that kindly modulated voice
Teaching Heaven's precepts to a youthful class
Which erst with statesman's eloquence controll'd
A different audience. The next holy day
Wondering beheld his place at church unfill'd,
And found him drooping in his peaceful home,
Guarded by tenderest love.

But on the third,
While the faint dawn was struggling to o'ercome
The lingering splendors of a full-orb'd moon,
The curtains of his tent were gently raised
And he had gone,—*gone*,—mourn'd by every heart
Among the people. They had seen in him
The truth personified, and felt the worth
Of such a Mentor.

'Twere impiety
To let the harp of praise in silence lie,
We who beheld so beautiful a life
Complete its perfect circle. Praise to Him
Who gave him power in Christ's dear name to pass
Unharm'd, the dangerous citadel of time,
Unsullied, o'er its countless snares to rise
From earthly care—to rest,—from war—to peace,—
From chance and change,—to everlasting bliss.
Give praise to God.

COLONEL H. L. MILLER,

Died at Hartford, December 30th, 1861.

SORROW and Joy collude. One mansion hears
The children shouting o'er their Christmas Tree,
While in the next resound the widow's wail
And weeping of the fatherless. So walk
Sickness and health. One rounds the cheek at morn,
The other with a ghost-like movement glides
Unto the nightly couch, and lo! the wheels
Of life drive heavily, and all its springs
Revolving in mysterious mechanism
Are troubled.
                                        And how slight the instrument
That sometimes sends the strong man to his tomb,
Revealing that the glory of his prime,
Is as the flower of grass.

                                        Of this we thought
When looking on the face that lay so calm
And comely in its narrow coffin-bed,
Remembering how the months of pain that sank
His manly vigor to an infant's sigh
Were met unmurmuringly.

Dense was the throng
That gather'd to his obsequies,—and well
The Pastor's prayer of faith essayed to gird
The smitten hearts that whelm'd in sorrow mourn'd
Husband and sire, whose ever-watchful love
Guarded their happiness.

Slowly moved on
The long procession, led by martial men
Who deeply in their patriot minds deplored
Their fallen compeer, and bade music lay
With plaintive voice, her chaplet down beside
His open grave.

Then, the first setting sun
Of our New-Year, cast off his wintry frown,
And seemed to write in clear, long lines of gold
Upon the whiten'd earth, the glorious words,
So shall the dead arise, at the last trump,
Sown here in weakness, to be raised in power,
Sown in corruption, to put on the robes
Of immortality.

Praise be to Him
Who gives through Christ our Lord, to dying flesh
Such victory.

COLONEL SAMUEL COLT,

Died at Hartford, on Friday morning, January 10th, 1862.

AND hath he fallen,—whom late we saw
  In manly vigor bold?
That stately form,—that noble face,
  Shall we no more behold?—
Not now of the renown we speak
  That gathers round his name,
For other climes beside our own
  Bear witness to his fame;

Nor of the high inventive power
  That stretched from zone to zone,
And 'neath the pathless ocean wrought,—
  For these to all are known;—
Nor of the love his liberal soul
  His native City bore,
For she hath monuments of this
  Till memory is no more;

Nor of the self-reliant force
  By which his way he told,
Nor of the Midas-touch that turn'd
  All enterprise to gold,
And made the indignant River yield
  Unto the ozier'd plain,—
For these would ask a wider range
  Than waits the lyric strain:

We choose those unobtrusive traits
  That dawn'd with influence mild,
When in his noble Mother's arms
  We saw the noble child,
And noted mid the changeful scenes
  Of boyhood's sport or strife,
That quiet, firm and ruling mind
  Which marked advancing life.

So onward as he held his course
  Through hardship to renown,
He kept fresh sympathy for those
  Who cope with fortune's frown,
The kind regard for honest toil,
  The joy to see it rise,
The fearless truth that never sought
  His frailties to disguise,

The lofty mind that all alone
  Gigantic plans sustain'd,
Yet turned unboastfully away
  From fame and honors gained;

The tender love for her who blest
  His home with angel-care,
And for the infant buds that rose
  In opening beauty fair.

Deep in the heart whence flows this lay,
  Is many a grateful trace
Of friendship's warm and earnest deed
  Which nought can e'er replace;
For in the glory of his prime
  The pulse forsakes his breast,
And by his buried little ones
  He lays him down to rest.

And thousand stand with drooping head
  Beside his open grave,
To whose industrious, faithful hands,
  The daily bread he gave,
The daily bread that wife and babe
  Or aged parent cheer'd,
Beneath the pleasant cottage roofs,
  Which he for them had rear'd.

There's mourning in the princely halls
  So late with gladness gay,
A tear within the heart of love
  That will not dry away;
A sense of loss on all around,
  A sigh of grief and pain—
"The like of him we lose to day,
  We ne'er shall see again."

MADAM HANNAH LATHROP,

Died in Norwich, Connecticut, January 18th, 1862, aged 92.

HAD I an artist's pencil, I might sketch
Her as she was, in her young matronhood
Graceful and dignified, serene and fair.

—I well remember, when at Sabbath-morn,
With pious zeal, the rural church she sought,
Our rural church,—by rocks o'er-canopied,—
Where with her stately husband and their group
Of younglings bright, each in the accustom'd seat,
How many a glance was toward her beauty bent
Admiringly.
In those primeval days
The aristocracy that won respect,
Sprang not from wealth alone, but laid its base
In goodness and in virtue. Thus she held
Her healthful influence in society
Without gainsaying voice.

The polity
Of woman's realm,—sweet home,—those inner cares
And countless details that promote its peace,
Prosperity and order, were not deem'd
Beneath the highest then, nor wholly left
To hireling hands. This science she upheld,
And with her circle of accomplishments
And charms so mingled it, that all combined
Harmoniously.
That energy and grace
So often deem'd the exclusive property
Of youth's fresh season, or of vigorous prime,
She brought to Age, an unencumbered dower,
Making the gift of being beautiful,
Even beyond ninety years.
And though the change
Of mortal life, dispers'd her cherish'd band,
And some had gone their own fair nests to build
And some arisen to mansions in the skies
Alone, yet undismay'd, her post she kept,
Guiding a household in the same good ways
Of order and of hospitality.

So, when with mild decline, the sunset came,
Her powers still unimpair'd, all willingly
As a confiding and obedient child
Goes to its father's house, she went above.

HENRIETTA SELDEN COLT,

Daughter of Col. SAMUEL and Mrs. ELIZABETH COLT, died January 20th, **1862**, aged 7 months and 27 days.

THE MOURNING MOTHER.

A TOMB for thee, my babe!
  Dove of my bosom, can it be?
But yesterday in all thy charms,
Laughing and leaping in my arms,
  A tomb and shroud for thee!

A couch for thee mine own,
  Beneath the frost and snow!
So fondly cradled, soft and warm,
And sheltered from each breath of storm,
  A wintry couch for thee!

Thy noble father's there,
  But the last week he died,
He would have stretched his guarding arm,
To shelter thee from every harm,
  Nestle thee to his side.

Thy ruby lip skill'd not
  That father's name to speak,
Yet wouldst thou pause mid infant play
To kiss his picture when away,
  The love smile on thy cheek.

Thy brother slumbereth there,
  Our first-born joy was he,
Thy little sister sweetly fair,
Most like a blessed bird of air;
  A goodly company.

Only one left with me,
  One here and *three* above,
Be not afraid my precious child!
The Shepherd of the lambs is mild,—
  Sleep in His love.

Thou never saw'st our Spring
  Unfold the blossoms gay;
But thou shalt see perennial bowers,
Enwreathed with bright and glorious flowers,
  That cannot fade away.

And thou shalt join the song,
  That happy cherubs pour,
In their adoring harmonies:
I'll hear ye, darlings, when I rise
  To that celestial shore.

Yes, there's a Saviour dear,—
  Keep down, oh tears, that swell!
A righteous God who reigns above,
Whose darkest ways are truth and love,
  He doeth all things well.

THE LITTLE BROTHERS.

WILLIAM CHILDS BREWER, died Jan. 24th, 1862, aged 7 years, and GEORGE CLEVELAND BREWER, aged 5 years, at Springfield, Mass., Feb. 4th, 1862.

THE noble boy amid his sports
Droop'd like a smitten flower
That feels the frost-king's fatal shaft,
And withers in its bower.

But then a younger darling sank
In childhood's rosy bloom,
And those whose hearts were one from birth,
Were brothers in the tomb.

Not in the tomb. Ah no! They rose
Through Christ their Saviour's love,
In his blest presence to cement
Their deathless bond of love.

Are they not dwelling side by side?
  Have they not 'scaped the strife,
The snares, the sins, the woes that stain
  This pilgrimage of life?

Oh heart of sorrowing Love, be strong!
  Tho' tenderest ties are riven,
For do not earth's bereavments aid
  The angel-chant of Heaven.

MR. DAVID F. ROBINSON,

Died at Hartford, January 26th, 1862, aged 61.

WE did not think it would be so;—
                                        We kept
The hope-lamp trimm'd and burning. Day by day
There came reports to cheer us;—and we thought
God in his goodness would not take away
So soon, another of that wasting band
Of worthies, whose example in our midst,
Precious and prized, we knew not how to spare.
These were our thoughts and prayers;—
                                But He who reigns
Above the clouds had different purposes.

On the low pillow where so late he mourn'd
His gifted first-born, in the prime of days,
Circled by all that makes life beautiful
And full of joy, his honored head is laid,—
The Sire and Son,—ne'er to be sunder'd more.

Yet his unblemish'd memory still survives,
And walks among us;—the upright intent,—
Firmness that conquer'd obstacles,—the zeal
For public good,—the warmth of charity,
And piety, that gave unwithering root
To every virtue.

Of the pleasant home
Where his most fond affections shed their balm
And found response,—now in its deep eclipse
And desolate, it is not ours to speak;
Nor by a powerless sympathy invade
The sacredness of grief.

'Twere fitter far
For faith to contemplate that glorious Home
Which knows no change, and lose itself in praise
Of Him, who to His faithful followers gives
Such blessed passport o'er the flood of Death,
That "where He is, there shall His servant be."

MR. SAMUEL TUDOR,

Died at Hartford, January 29th, 1862, aged 92.

We saw him on a winter's day,
  Beneath the hallowed dome,
Where for so many years his heart
  Had found its Sabbath-home,
Yet not amid his ancient seat
  Or in the accustomed place
Arose his fair, and reverend brow,
  And form of manly grace.

Then Music, through the organ's soul
  Melodious descant gave,
But yet his voice so rich and sweet
  Swell'd not the sacred stave,
The Christmas wreaths o'er arch and nave
  Were lingering still to cheer
His parting visit to the fane
  Which he had help'd to rear.

And flowers were on the coffin-lid
  And o'er his bosom strown,
Fit offering for the friend who loved
  The plants of every zone,
And bade them in his favor'd cell
  Unfold their charms sublime,
And felt the florist's genial joy
  Repel the frost of time.

No cloud of sorrow marr'd his course,
  Save when *her* loss he wept,
Whose image in his constant soul
  Its angel presence kept,
But heavenly Mercy's balm was shed
  To cheer his lonely breast,
For tenderest love in filial hearts
  His latest moments blest.

And so, for more than ninety years
  Flow'd on his cloudless span,
In love of Nature, and of Art,
  And kindred love for man,
Our oldest patriarch, kind and true,
  To all our City dear,
His cordial tones, his greeting words
  No more on earth we hear.

Last of that band of noble men
  Who for their Church's weal

Took counsel in her hour of need
  And wrought with tireless zeal,
Nor in their fervent toil declined
  Nor loiter'd on their ways,
Until her Gothic towers arose
  And her full chant of praise.

But as we laid him down with tears,
  The westering Sun shone bright,
And through the ice-clad evergreens
  Diffused prismatic light,
Type of the glory that awaits
  The rising of the just,
And so, we left him in the grave
  That Christ his Lord had blest.

HENRY HOWARD COMSTOCK,

Youngest child of the late Capt. JOHN C. COMSTOCK, died at Hartford, February 11th, 1862, a fortnight after his father, aged 11 months.

IT was a fair and mournful sight
  Once at the wintry tide,
When to the dear baptismal rite
Was brought an infant, sweet and bright,
  His father's couch beside,

His dying father's couch beside,
  Whose eye, with tranquil ray,
Beheld upon that beauteous head
The consecrated water shed,
  Then calmly pass'd away.

A little while the lovely babe,
  As if by angels lent,
With soft caress and soothing wile
Invok'd a widow'd mother's smile,
  Then to his father went.

Christ's holy seal upon his brow,
  Christ's sign upon his breast,
He 'scaped from all the cares and woes
That earth inflicts or manhood knows,
  And enter'd with the blest.

REV. DR. DAVID SMITH,

For many years Pastor of a Church in Durham, Conn., died at Fair Haven, March 3d, 1862, aged 94.

THE transcript of a long, unblemish'd life
Replete with happiness and holiness,
Is a fair page to look upon with love
In this world's volume oft defaced by sin,
And marr'd with misery. And he, who laid
His earthly vestments down this day, doth leave
Such tablet for the heart.
'Twas good to see
That what he preach'd to others, he portray'd
Before them in example, that the eye
Adding its stronger comment to the ear,
Might lend new impulse to the flock he led
Toward the Great Shepherd's fold.

Along his path
Sorrows he met, but such as wrought him gain,

And joys that made not weak his hold on heaven,
But touch'd his brow with sunbeams, and his heart
With warmer charity.
Year after year,
Home's duties and its hospitalities
Were blent with cheerfulness, and when the chill
Of hoary Time approach'd he took no part
In that repulsive criticism of age,
Pronouncing with a frown, the former days
Better than these.
The florid glow that tints
The cheek of health, which youth perchance, accounts
Its own peculiar beauty, dwelt with him
Till more than fourscore years and ten achiev'd
Their patriarch circle, while the pleasant smile
And genial manner, casting light around
His venerable age, conspired to make
His company desirable to all.

And so beloved on earth and waited for
Above, he closed this mortal pilgrimage
In perfect peace.

MISS. EMILY B. PARISH,

Formerly a Teacher in Hartford, died at Cleveland, Ohio, March 12th, 1862.

TEACHERS,—she is not here
  With the first breath of Spring
Her aid to your devoted band
With cheering smile and ready hand
  Untiringly to bring.

Pupils,—her guiding voice,
  Her sweetly warbled strain
Urging your spirits to be wise
With daily, tuneful harmonies
  Ye shall not hear again.

Parents,—and loving friends
  The parents' heart who shared,
Give thanks to that abounding grace
Which led her through the Christian race,
  To find its high reward.

Lover,—the spell is broke
  That o'er your life she wove,
Look to her flitting robes that gleam
So white, beyond cold Jordan's stream,
  Look to the Land of Love.

HARRIET ALLEN ELY,

Died at Providence, Rhode Island, April 27th, 1862, aged 7 years and 2 months.

SEVEN blest years our darling daughter,
We have held thee to our hearts,
Every season growing dearer;
We have held thee near and nearer,
Never dreaming thus to part.

Seven brief years—our only daughter—
Sweet has been the parent rule,
Infant watch by cradle nightly,
'Till we saw thy footsteps lightly
Tripping joyously to school.

Germ of promise,—bud of beauty,
To our tenderest nurture given,
Not for our too dim beholding
Was thy fair and full unfolding;
That perfection is in Heaven.

Earth no license had to harm thee,
Time no power to touch thy bloom,
Holy is our faith to meet thee,
Glorious is our trust to greet thee
Far beyond the conquering tomb.

MISS CATHARINE BALL,

Daughter of Hon. Judge BALL of Hoosick Falls, N. Y., died at the City of Washington, 1862.

BRIGHT sunbeam of a father's heart
  Whose earliest radiance shone
Delightful o'er a mother's eye
Like morning-star in cloudless sky,
  Say, whither hast thou flown?

Fair inmate of a happy home
  Whose love so gently shed
Could a serene enchantment make
And love in stranger bosoms wake,
  Ah, whither art thou fled?

They know, who trust the Saviour's word
  With faith no tear can dim,
That such as bear His spirit here
And do His will in duty's sphere
  Shall rise to dwell with Him.

They know, who feel an Angel near,
  Though hid from mortal sight
And reaching out to her their hand
Shall safer reach that Pleasant Land
  Whose buds no blast can blight.

Even I, who but with fleeting glance
  Beheld thee here below,
From its remembered sweetness gain
New impulse toward that heavenly train
Whose harps in never-ceasing strain
  With God's high praises glow.

MRS. MORRIS COLLINS,

Died at Hartford, May 19th, 1862.

FRAIL stranger at the gate of life,
  Too weak to grasp its key,
O'er whom the Sun on car of gold
Hath but a few times risen and roll'd,
  Unnoticed still by thee,—

To whom the toil of breath is new,
  In this our vale of time
Whose feet are yet unskill'd to tread
The grassy carpet round thee spread
  At the soft, vernal prime,—

Deep sympathy and pitying care
  Regard thy helpless moan,
And 'neath thy forehead arching high
Methinks, the brightly opening eye
  Doth search for something gone.

Yon slumberer 'mid the snowy flowers,
With young, unfrosted hair,
Awakes not at the mournful sound
Of bird-like voices murmuring round
"*Why sleeps our Mother there?*"

Hers was that sunshine of the heart,
Which Home's fair region cheer'd,
Hers the upright, unselfish aim,
The fond response to duty's claim,
The faith that never fear'd.

Oh mystery! brooding oft so dark
O'er this our path below,
Not ours, with wild, repining sigh,
To ask the *wherefore*, or the *why*,
But drink our cup of woe.

So, in her shrouded beauty cold,
Yield to the earth its own,
Assured that Heaven will guard the trust,
Of that which may not turn to dust,
But dwells beside the Throne.

MRS. MARGARET WALBRIDGE,

Died at Saratoga, N. Y., June 2d, 1862, aged 35.

WRITTEN ON HER BIRTH-DAY.

THIS was her birth-day here,
When summer's latest flowers
Were kindling to their flush and prime,
As if they felt how short the time
In these terrestrial bowers.

She hath a birth-day now
No hastening night that knows,
She hath a never-ending year
Which feels no blight of autumn sere,
Nor chill of wintry snows.

She hath no pain or fear,
But by her Saviour's side
Expansion finds for every power;
And knowledge her angelic dower
An ever-flowing tide.

They sorrow, who were called
  From her sweet smile to part,
Who wore her love-links fondly twined
Like woven threads of gold refined
  Around their inmost heart.

Tears are upon the cheeks
  Of little ones this day,
God of the motherless,—whose eye
Notes even the ravens when they cry
  Wipe Thou their tears away:

Oh, comfort all who grieve
  Beside the sacred urn,—
For brief our space to wail or sigh,
Like grass we fade, like dreams we fly,
  And rest with those we mourn.

THE BROTHERS.

Mr. FISHER AMES BUELL, died at Hartford, May 19th, 1861, aged 25, and Mr. HENRY R. BUELL, on his voyage to Europe, June 20th, 1862, aged 30, the only children of Mr. ROBERT and Mrs. LAURA BUELL.

Both gone. Both smitten in their manly prime,
Yet the fair transcript of their virtues here,
And treasured memories of their boyhood's time
Allay the anguish of affection's tear.

One hath his rest amid the sacred shade
Whose turf reveals the mourner's frequent tread,
And one beneath the unfathomed deep is laid
To slumber till the sea restores her dead.

The childless parents weep their broken trust,
Hope's fountain failing at its cherish'd springs,
And widow'd sorrow shrouds herself in dust,
While one lone flowret to her bosom clings.

Yet no blind chance this saddening change hath wrought,
No dark misrule this mortal life attends,
A Heavenly Father's never-erring thought
Commingles with the discipline He sends.

Not for His reasons let us dare to ask,
  His secret counsels not aspire to read,
But faithful bow to each allotted task
  And make His will our solace and our creed.

HON. PHILLIP RIPLEY,

Died at Hartford, July 8th, 1862, aged 68.

It is not meet the good and just
  Oblivious pass away,
And leave no record for their race,
Except a dim and fading trace,
  The memory of a day.

We need the annal of their course,
  Their pattern for a guide,—
Their armor that temptation quell'd,—
The beacon-light that forth they held
  O'er Time's delusive tide.

Within the House of God I sate
  At Summer's morning ray,—
And sadly mark'd a vacant seat
Where erst in storm, or cold or heat
  While lustrums held their way,

Was ever seen with reverent air
  Intent on hallow'd lore,
A forehead edg'd with silver hair,
A manly form bow'd low in prayer,—
  They greet our eyes no more.

And where *Philanthropy commands
  Her lighted lamp to burn,
And youthful feet inured to stray
Are wisely warn'd to duty's way,
  Repentant to return,

He, with a faith that never fail'd,
  Its first inception blest,—
And year by year, with zeal untired,
Wise counsel lent,—new hopes inspired,
  And righteous precepts prest.

They did him honor at his grave,
  Those men of mystic sign,
Whose ancient symbols bright and fair,
The Book, the Level, and the Square,
  Betoken truth benign:

All do him honor, who regard
  Integrity sincere,
But they who knew his virtues best,
While fond remembrance rules the breast,
  Will hold his image dear.

---

* Mr. Ripley was a persevering friend and patron of the State Reform School at West Meriden. He had long sustained the office of Trustee for the County of Hartford, and was at the time of his death, the Chairman of that body, and a prominent member of its Executive Committee. His frequent visits to that Institution, his attention to all its internal concerns, and earnest satisfaction in its prosperity, entitle him to its grateful remembrance.

RICHARD ELY COLLINS,

Son of Mr. MORRIS COLLINS, died at Wethersfield, September 5th, 1862, aged 3 months and 27 days.

IT was a sad and lovely sight
 They call'd us to behold,
That infant forehead high and fair,
Those beauteous features sculptured rare,
 Yet breathless all, and cold.

Heard it in dreams, an angel voice
 Soft as the zephyr's tone?
The yearning of a Mother mild
To clasp once more her three months' child
 But a few days her own?

Just a few days of wasting pain
 She linger'd by its side,
And then consign'd to stranger arms
The frail unfolding of the charms
 She would have watch'd with pride.

Yet happy babe! to reach a home
  Beyond all sorrowing cares,
Where none a Mother's loss can moan
Or seek for bread, and find a stone,
  Or fall in fatal snares.

Thrice happy,—to have pass'd away
  Ere Time's sore ills invade,—
From fragrant buds that drooping shed
Their life-sigh o'er thy coffin-bed—
  To flowers that never fade.

MISS ELIZABETH BRINLEY,

Died at Hartford, September 28th, 1862.

WE miss her at the chancel-side,
  For when we last drew near,
The holy Eucharist to share,
She, with the warmth of praise and prayer
  Was meekly kneeling here.

We miss her when the liberal hand
  Relieves a thirsting soil,
And when the Blessed Church demands
Assistance for the mission bands
  That on her frontier toil.

We miss her 'mid the gather'd train
  Of children* young and poor,
Whom year by year she deign'd to teach
With faithful zeal and patient speech,
  And hope that anchor'd sure.

Her couch is in the ancestral tomb
   With Putnam's honor'd dust,
The true in word, the bold in deed,
A bulwark in his Country's need,
   A tower of strength and trust.

Her spirit's home is with her Lord,
   Whom from her youth she sought,
The miss'd below hath found above
The promise of a God of Love
   Made to the pure in thought.

---

* The well-conducted Industrial School in connection with St. Paul's Church, where she had been for several years an indefatigable and valued teacher.

MR. JOHN A. TAINTOR,

Died at Hartford, on Saturday Evening, November 15th, 1862, aged 62 years.

A SENSE of loss is on us. One hath gone
Whose all-pervading energy doth leave
A void and silence 'mid the haunts of men
And desolation for the hearts that grieve
In his fair mansion, so bereft and lone,
Whence the inspiring smile, and cheering voice have flown.

Those too there are who eloquently speak
Of his firm friendship, not without a tear,
Of its strong power to undergird the weak
And hold the faltering feet in duty's sphere,
While in the cells of want, a broken trust
In bitterness laments, that he is of the dust.

In foreign climes, with patriotic eye
He sought what might his Country's welfare aid,
And the rich flocks of Spain, at his behest
Spread their proud fleeces o'er our verdant glade,
And Scotia's herds, as on their native shore
Our never-failing streams, and pastures rich explore.

Intent was he to adorn his own domain
  With all the radiant charms that Flora brings,
There still, the green-house flowers pronounce his name,
  The favor'd rose its grateful fragrance flings,
And in their faithful ranks to guard the scene
Like changeless memories rise, the unfading evergreen.

On friendly deeds intent, while on his way
  A widow'd heart to cheer,—*One* grasp'd his hand
Whose icy touch the beating heart can stay,
  And in a moment, at that stern command
Unwarn'd, yet not unready, he doth show
The great transition made, that waits on all below.

Yet, ah! the contrast,—when the form that pass'd
  Forth from its gates, in full vitality,
Is homeward, as a lifeless burden borne,
  No more to breathe kind word, or fond reply,
Each nameless care assume with earnest skill,
Nor the unspoken wish of those he loved fulfill.

But hallow'd lips within the sacred dome
  Where he so long his sabbath-worship paid
Have given his soul to God from whence it came
  And laid his head beneath the cypress shade,
While "*be ye also ready*," from his tomb,
In a Redeemer's voice, doth neutralize the gloom.

www.ingramcontent.com/pod-product-compliance
Lightning Source LLC
LaVergne TN
LVHW010232110826
845151LV00004B/1274
9781425524852